JOSHUA BRUCE

The Ultimate Job Interview Playbook

Master 100 Powerful Questions, Winning Answers, and Expert Strategies Time Tested and Proven to keep you on the KNOW in every interview

Copyright © 2024 by Joshua Bruce

All rights reserved. No part of this publication may be reproduced, stored or transmitted in any form or by any means, electronic, mechanical, photocopying, recording, scanning, or otherwise without written permission from the publisher. It is illegal to copy this book, post it to a website, or distribute it by any other means without permission.

First edition

This book was professionally typeset on Reedsy.
Find out more at reedsy.com

Contents

Introduction: The Interview Game Changer	1
1. The Psychology of Job Interviews: Mindset and Preparation	6
2. The 20 Most Common Interview Questions and How to Ace...	12
3. Behavioral Questions: Proving Your Worth with the STAR...	19
4. Situational and Problem-Solving Questions: Showcasing...	25
5. Technical and Industry-Specific Questions: Demonstrating...	31
6. Leadership and Management Questions: For Career...	38
7. Curve ball Questions: Handling the Unexpected with...	45
8. Questions for Career Changers and Fresh Graduates	52
9. Crafting Memorable Answers: Tailoring Your Responses	58
10. Turning Weaknesses into Strengths: The Art of Positive...	65
11. Quantifying Your Achievements for Maximum Impact	72
12. Body Language and Non-Verbal Communication in Interviews	80
13. Mastering the Art of Storytelling in Your Responses	88
14. Acing Different Interview Formats: One-on-One, Panel,...	95
15. The Post-Interview Playbook: Following Up and...	102
16. Industry-Specific Interview Guides: Tech, Finance,...	108
17. 25 Smart Questions to Ask Your Interviewer	117
18. The Ultimate Interview Toolkit: Checklist, Power Words,...	124
19. Overcoming Interview Anxiety: Techniques for Staying...	132
20. Building Your Personal Brand: Resume, Cover Letter, and...	139
Conclusion: Your Journey to Interview Excellence	146
Chapter 23	153

Introduction: The Interview Game Changer

In today's competitive job market, landing your dream job often hinges on a single, crucial event: the interview. It's a high-stakes game where every word, every gesture, and every response can tip the scales in your favor—or against you. But what if you could walk into every interview with the confidence of a seasoned pro? What if you could anticipate the questions, craft compelling answers, and leave a lasting impression that sets you apart from the crowd?

Welcome to "Ace Any Interview," your comprehensive guide to mastering the art and science of job interviews. This book isn't just another collection of generic advice; it's a game-changer designed to transform your approach to interviews and dramatically increase your chances of success.

The Power of Preparation

Think back to your last job interview. Did you feel fully prepared, or were you scrambling to come up with answers on the spot? Did you leave feeling confident, or did you spend hours afterward thinking of all the things you should have said? If you're like most people, interviews can be a source of stress and uncertainty. But it doesn't have to be this way.

The secret to interview success isn't some innate talent or stroke of luck—it's preparation. Thorough, strategic, and focused preparation. This book will show you how to prepare not just adequately, but exceptionally. You'll learn how to anticipate the questions you'll face, craft responses that highlight your unique value, and present yourself as the ideal candidate for the job.

Why This Book Is Different

The job market is flooded with interview guides, so why should you choose this one? Because "Ace Any Interview" goes beyond the basics to offer you:

1. Comprehensive Coverage: We've analyzed thousands of real-world interviews across various industries to bring you the 100 most impactful questions you're likely to face. But we don't stop at just listing questions—we provide in-depth strategies for crafting powerful answers.

2. Psychological Insights: Understanding the psychology behind interview questions is crucial. We delve into why interviewers ask certain questions and what they're really looking for in your answers. This insight allows you to tailor your responses for maximum impact.

3. Industry-Specific Guidance: Whether you're in tech, finance, healthcare, or any other field, you'll find tailored advice to help you shine in your specific industry.

4. Practical Strategies: From the STAR method for behavioral questions to techniques for handling curveballs, you'll gain actionable strategies you can apply immediately.

5. Holistic Approach: We cover every aspect of the interview process, from pre-interview preparation to post-interview follow-up, ensuring you're equipped for success at every stage.

The Evolution of Job Interviews

INTRODUCTION: THE INTERVIEW GAME CHANGER

To truly excel in modern interviews, it's essential to understand how they've evolved. Gone are the days when interviews were simple Q&A sessions about your resume. Today's interviews are complex evaluations of not just your skills and experience, but your personality, problem-solving abilities, cultural fit, and potential for growth.

Behavioral and situational questions have become increasingly common, requiring candidates to provide specific examples of past performance or hypothetical responses to work scenarios. Technical interviews, particularly in fields like IT and engineering, often include practical tests or coding challenges. And with the rise of remote work, video interviews have introduced a new set of challenges and opportunities.

This book is designed with these evolutions in mind, preparing you for the full spectrum of modern interview techniques and formats.

The 80/20 Rule of Interview Success

You've likely heard of the Pareto Principle, or the 80/20 rule, which states that roughly 80% of effects come from 20% of causes. This principle applies surprisingly well to job interviews. While there are countless potential questions an interviewer might ask, we've found that mastering responses to about 20% of common questions can prepare you for 80% of what you're likely to face.

This book focuses on that crucial 20%—the questions and techniques that will give you the most significant return on your preparation time. By deeply understanding and practicing these core elements, you'll be well-equipped to handle whatever comes your way in the interview.

Beyond Questions and Answers

While a significant portion of this book is dedicated to specific questions and strategies for answering them, interviewing excellence goes beyond mere Q&A. That's why we also cover critical topics like:

- Body language and non-verbal communication
    - The art of storytelling in interviews
    - Building rapport with your interviewer
    - Strategies for different interview formats (one-on-one, panel, video)
    - Post-interview follow-up and salary negotiation

By mastering these additional elements, you'll elevate your interview performance from good to exceptional.

The Confidence Factor

One of the most significant benefits of thorough preparation is the confidence it instills. When you walk into an interview knowing you've done the work—that you've anticipated the questions, crafted compelling stories, and aligned your experiences with the job requirements—it shows. This confidence is palpable to interviewers and can be the deciding factor in their hiring decision.

Throughout this book, we'll provide not just knowledge, but also techniques to boost your confidence and manage interview anxiety. Because when you feel confident, you perform at your best.

Your Journey to Interview Excellence

As you embark on this journey to interview mastery, remember that improvement is a process. Each chapter of this book builds upon the last, providing you with a comprehensive framework for interview success. We encourage you to not just read, but to actively engage with the material:

- Practice the sample answers out loud

INTRODUCTION: THE INTERVIEW GAME CHANGER

- Customize the strategies to fit your unique experiences
- Use the end-of-chapter exercises to reinforce your learning
- Leverage the online resources for continued growth and updates

Your Path Forward

Whether you're a fresh graduate looking for your first job, a seasoned professional aiming for a career change, or someone climbing the corporate ladder, this book is your roadmap to interview success. By the time you finish "Ace Any Interview," you'll have the tools, strategies, and confidence to tackle any interview that comes your way.

Remember, every great career starts with a successful interview. Let's begin your journey to mastering the art of interviewing and unlocking the career of your dreams.

Are you ready to become an interview ace? Let's dive in.

1. The Psychology of Job Interviews: Mindset and Preparation

Job interviews are more than just a question-and-answer session; they're a complex psychological dance between interviewer and candidate. Understanding the mental dynamics at play can give you a significant edge in your next interview. This chapter will explore the psychology behind job interviews and provide you with strategies to prepare your mindset for optimal performance.

The Interviewer's Perspective

To excel in interviews, it's crucial to understand what's going on in the interviewer's mind. Their primary goals are:

1. Assessing Competence: They want to ensure you have the skills and knowledge required for the role.
2. Evaluating Cultural Fit: They're determining if you'll mesh well with the team and company culture.
3. Gauging Motivation: They want to understand your drive and commitment to the role and organization.
4. Predicting Future Performance: They're trying to forecast how you'll perform based on past experiences and current attitudes.

1. THE PSYCHOLOGY OF JOB INTERVIEWS: MINDSET AND PREPARATION

By understanding these objectives, you can frame your responses strategically, addressing the underlying concerns of the interviewer. For example, when discussing your experiences, don't just focus on what you did, but also on how it benefited your previous employer and how it aligns with the prospective role.

The Candidate's Psychology

As a candidate, you're likely to face several psychological challenges:

1. Anxiety and Stress: It's normal to feel nervous before and during an interview. The key is managing these feelings so they don't impair your performance. Practice deep breathing exercises or progressive muscle relaxation techniques to calm your nerves. Remember, a moderate level of anxiety can actually enhance your performance by keeping you alert and focused.

2. Imposter Syndrome: Many candidates, even highly qualified ones, suffer from feelings of self-doubt. Combat this by objectively reviewing your achievements and qualifications. Remind yourself of specific instances where you've succeeded in similar situations.

3. Cognitive Biases: We all have inherent biases that can affect our performance. For instance, the spotlight effect might make you overestimate how much the interviewer is focusing on your every move, leading to unnecessary stress. Being aware of these biases can help you mitigate their effects.

Mindset Preparation

Cultivating the right mindset is crucial for interview success. Here are key areas to focus on:

1. Growth Mindset: Adopt a growth mindset, viewing the interview as an opportunity for learning and improvement, regardless of the outcome. This approach can help you stay positive and resilient, even if you face challenging questions or unexpected situations.

2. Positive Self-Talk: The way you talk to yourself has a significant impact on your confidence and performance. Practice positive affirmations and reframe negative thoughts. Instead of thinking, "I'm not qualified for this job," try, "I have unique experiences that can bring value to this role."

3. Resilience: Build mental toughness to bounce back from setbacks or tough questions. Remember that one difficult moment doesn't define the entire interview. Prepare a mental reset button to quickly recover and refocus if you feel you've stumbled.

The Power of First Impressions

In interviews, first impressions matter significantly. Here's what you need to know:

1. The Halo Effect: This psychological phenomenon shows that a positive first impression can influence the overall perception of a person. Make a strong entrance with confident body language, a warm smile, and a firm handshake (when appropriate).

2. Nonverbal Cues: Your body language speaks volumes. Maintain good posture, make appropriate eye contact, and use gestures naturally to emphasize your points. Be aware of nervous habits like fidgeting or playing with your hair, as these can distract from your message.

3. Rapport Building: Quickly establishing a positive connection with the interviewer can set a favorable tone for the entire interview. Find common ground through small talk, show genuine interest in the interviewer's

1. THE PSYCHOLOGY OF JOB INTERVIEWS: MINDSET AND PREPARATION

perspective, and mirror their communication style subtly.

Preparation Strategies

Effective preparation goes beyond rehearsing answers. It's about getting your mind ready for peak performance:

1. Mental Rehearsal: Use visualization techniques to imagine a successful interview. Picture yourself answering questions confidently, building rapport with the interviewer, and leaving a strong positive impression. This mental practice can boost your confidence and performance.

2. Knowledge is Power: Thoroughly researching the company, role, and industry not only prepares you to answer questions but also reduces anxiety. The more you know, the more confident you'll feel.

3. The Confidence-Competence Loop: As you prepare and practice, you'll build both skills and confidence. This creates a positive feedback loop: the more competent you become, the more confident you feel, which in turn enhances your performance.

Handling Unexpected Situations

No matter how well you prepare, you may encounter unexpected questions or situations. Here's how to ready your mind:

1. Cognitive Flexibility: Develop the ability to think on your feet by practicing impromptu speaking. Try answering random questions on the spot or participating in debate-style discussions with friends.

2. Stress Inoculation: Expose yourself to stressful interview scenarios in a controlled environment. Ask a friend to conduct a mock interview with particularly challenging questions. This practice can help you build resilience

and stay calm under pressure.

3. Reframing Techniques: Learn to reframe potentially negative situations into opportunities. If you're asked about a weakness, for instance, discuss it briefly but focus on the steps you're taking to improve.

The Role of Authenticity

While preparation is crucial, it's equally important to remain authentic:

1. The Authenticity Paradox: Over-rehearsing can make you sound robotic or insincere. Strike a balance by internalizing key points rather than memorizing scripts verbatim.

2. Values Alignment: Identify your core values and look for ways to authentically express them in relation to the job and company. This alignment can help you connect more genuinely with the interviewer and the role.

3. Storytelling with Integrity: Craft compelling narratives about your experiences that are both strategic and true. Use the STAR method (Situation, Task, Action, Result) to structure your stories, ensuring they're relevant and impactful.

Conclusion

Mastering the psychology of job interviews is about more than just knowing what to say. It's about preparing your mind to perform at its best under pressure. By understanding the psychological dynamics at play, cultivating the right mindset, and practicing effective preparation strategies, you can enter your next interview with confidence, authenticity, and the mental agility to handle whatever comes your way.

Remember, every interview is an opportunity – not just for landing a job,

1. THE PSYCHOLOGY OF JOB INTERVIEWS: MINDSET AND PREPARATION

but for personal growth and self-discovery. Approach each one with a learner's mindset, and you'll find yourself not just succeeding in interviews, but thriving in your career journey.

2. The 20 Most Common Interview Questions and How to Ace Them

Mastering the most common interview questions is crucial for interview success. While every interview is unique, certain questions appear with remarkable consistency across industries and job levels. In this chapter, we'll explore the 20 most common interview questions and provide strategies to craft compelling answers that will set you apart from other candidates.

1. "Tell me about yourself."

This open-ended question often serves as an icebreaker but is also a critical opportunity to make a strong first impression.

Strategy: Craft a concise "elevator pitch" that highlights your professional journey, key achievements, and what drives you. Focus on relevant experiences and skills that align with the job description. End with a statement that bridges your background to the role you're interviewing for.

Example: "I'm a marketing professional with 7 years of experience in digital strategy. I've led campaigns that increased client engagement by 40% and drove $2M in new revenue. I'm passionate about data-driven marketing and am excited about the opportunity to bring my expertise to your growing e-commerce division."

2. THE 20 MOST COMMON INTERVIEW QUESTIONS AND HOW TO ACE...

2. "Why do you want to work here?"

This question assesses your knowledge of the company and your genuine interest in the role.

Strategy: Research the company thoroughly. Highlight specific aspects of the company's mission, culture, or recent projects that resonate with you. Connect these elements to your career goals and values.

3. "What are your greatest strengths?"

Here, the interviewer wants to understand how your strengths align with the job requirements.

Strategy: Choose 2-3 strengths that are directly relevant to the position. Provide specific examples of how you've utilized these strengths to achieve results in past roles.

4. "What is your greatest weakness?"

This question tests your self-awareness and ability to improve.

Strategy: Choose a genuine weakness, but one that isn't central to the job. More importantly, focus on the steps you're taking to overcome this weakness.

Example: "I sometimes struggle with public speaking. To address this, I've joined a local Toastmasters group and have been volunteering to lead more presentations at work. I've already seen significant improvement in my confidence and delivery."

5. "Where do you see yourself in five years?"

Employers want to gauge your ambition and whether your goals align with their long-term needs.

Strategy: Be honest about your career aspirations while demonstrating how they could align with the company's growth. Show enthusiasm for growing within the organization.

6. "Can you describe a challenging work situation and how you overcame it?"

This behavioral question assesses your problem-solving skills and resilience.

Strategy: Use the STAR method (Situation, Task, Action, Result) to structure your response. Choose a situation that highlights your ability to handle challenges relevant to the role you're applying for.

7. "Why are you leaving your current job?"

Interviewers want to understand your motivations and ensure you're not a flight risk.

Strategy: Stay positive and focus on what you're moving towards rather than what you're leaving behind. Emphasize growth opportunities and new challenges you're seeking.

8. "What's your leadership style?"

Even for non-managerial positions, this question gauges your ability to influence and work with others.

Strategy: Describe your approach to leading or collaborating with others. Provide an example of when your leadership style was effective in achieving a team goal.

2. THE 20 MOST COMMON INTERVIEW QUESTIONS AND HOW TO ACE...

9. "How do you handle stress and pressure?"

Employers want to ensure you can perform under challenging conditions.

Strategy: Describe specific techniques you use to manage stress. Provide an example of a high-pressure situation you handled successfully.

10. "What are your salary expectations?"

This question can be tricky, as you don't want to price yourself out or undervalue your worth.

Strategy: Research industry standards for the role and your experience level. Provide a range rather than a specific number, and express openness to negotiation based on the total compensation package.

11. "Why should we hire you?"

This is your chance to make a compelling case for yourself.

Strategy: Summarize your most relevant skills and experiences. Highlight what sets you apart from other candidates and how you can contribute to the company's goals.

12. "Do you have any questions for us?"

This is not just a courtesy; it's an opportunity to demonstrate your interest and insight.

Strategy: Prepare thoughtful questions about the role, team dynamics, company culture, and future plans. Avoid questions about basic information readily available on the company website.

13. "Describe a time when you disagreed with a supervisor."

This question assesses your ability to handle conflict professionally.

Strategy: Choose an example where you navigated the disagreement constructively. Emphasize your communication skills and willingness to find common ground.

14. "How do you stay organized and manage your time?"

Employers want to know that you can handle multiple responsibilities efficiently.

Strategy: Describe specific tools or techniques you use (e.g., project management software, to-do lists). Provide an example of how your organizational skills improved efficiency in a previous role.

15. "What's your ideal work environment?"

This question helps assess your fit with the company culture.

Strategy: Be honest about your preferences, but also demonstrate flexibility. Research the company culture beforehand and highlight aspects that align with your ideal.

16. "How do you keep your skills current?"

Employers value candidates who are committed to continuous learning.

Strategy: Discuss professional development activities you engage in, such as online courses, industry conferences, or relevant reading. Show enthusiasm for staying updated in your field.

2. THE 20 MOST COMMON INTERVIEW QUESTIONS AND HOW TO ACE...

17. "Can you explain this gap in your employment history?"

If applicable, be prepared to address any career breaks transparently.

Strategy: Be honest and focus on any positive outcomes or learnings from the gap period. If you acquired new skills or engaged in volunteer work, mention these.

18. "What's the most interesting project you've worked on?"

This question allows you to showcase your passion and achievements.

Strategy: Choose a project that demonstrates skills relevant to the job you're applying for. Explain your role, the challenges you faced, and the impact of the project.

19. "How do you handle failure?"

Employers want to see resilience and a growth mindset.

Strategy: Describe a specific failure, what you learned from it, and how you applied that learning to achieve success in a subsequent situation.

20. "What motivates you?"

This question helps employers understand what drives you and how to keep you engaged.

Strategy: Be genuine in your response. Connect your motivations to aspects of the job or company mission to show alignment.

Conclusion

Preparing for these common questions is essential, but remember that authenticity is key. Your goal is not to memorize scripted answers but to internalize the key points you want to convey. This allows you to respond naturally while ensuring you hit the important notes.

Practice your responses out loud, ideally with a friend or mentor who can provide feedback. Pay attention to your body language and tone as well as your words. With thorough preparation and a confident mindset, you'll be well-equipped to ace these common interview questions and make a lasting impression on your potential employer.

Remember, the best interviews feel like natural conversations. Use these prepared responses as a foundation, but be ready to engage in a genuine dialogue with your interviewer. Your authentic self, combined with thoughtful preparation, is your most powerful tool in any interview situation.

3. Behavioral Questions: Proving Your Worth with the STAR Method

Behavioral questions have become a cornerstone of modern interviewing techniques. These questions ask you to provide specific examples of how you've handled situations in the past, based on the premise that past behavior is the best predictor of future performance. Mastering these questions is crucial for interview success, and the STAR method is your key to crafting compelling, concise, and relevant responses.

Understanding Behavioral Questions

Behavioral questions typically start with phrases like:
  - "Tell me about a time when…"
  - "Describe a situation where…"
  - "Give me an example of…"

These questions aim to uncover how you've actually behaved in real situations, rather than how you think you might behave in hypothetical scenarios. They probe various competencies, including:

- Leadership
   - Teamwork
   - Problem-solving
   - Conflict resolution

- Adaptability
- Time management
- Communication skills

Interviewers use these questions to assess whether you have the specific skills and experiences required for the role.

The STAR Method: Your Framework for Success

STAR stands for Situation, Task, Action, and Result. This method provides a structured approach to answering behavioral questions effectively:

Situation: Set the scene and provide context for your story.
   Task: Explain your responsibility in that situation.
   Action: Describe the steps you took to address the situation.
   Result: Share the outcomes of your actions.

Let's break down each component:

Situation:
   Provide a concise overview of the event or circumstance. Include enough detail to paint a clear picture, but don't get bogged down in unnecessary information. Mention where and when the situation occurred, and why it was challenging or important.

Task:
   Explain your specific role or responsibility in the situation. What was expected of you? What goal were you working toward?

Action:
   This is the meat of your response. Detail the specific steps you took to address the situation. Focus on your individual contributions, even if you were part of a team. Use "I" statements to clarify your personal actions.

3. BEHAVIORAL QUESTIONS: PROVING YOUR WORTH WITH THE STAR...

Result:

Describe the outcome of your actions. Quantify the results whenever possible (e.g., "increased efficiency by 25%," "reduced costs by $10,000"). If the outcome was not entirely positive, explain what you learned and how you'd approach a similar situation differently in the future.

Implementing the STAR Method: An Example

Let's apply the STAR method to a common behavioral question: "Tell me about a time when you had to deal with a difficult team member."

Situation: "In my previous role as a project manager at XYZ Corp, we were working on a critical software update with a tight six-week deadline. One team member, a senior developer, consistently missed internal deadlines and was often defensive when asked about his progress."

Task: "As the project manager, it was my responsibility to ensure all team members were on track and to address any issues that could jeopardize our deadline."

Action: "I scheduled a one-on-one meeting with the developer to understand the root of the problem. I discovered he was struggling with a particularly complex coding issue and felt embarrassed to ask for help. I assured him that seeking assistance was not a sign of weakness but a normal part of the development process.

I then reorganized our team structure to pair him with another experienced developer who could provide guidance. I also implemented daily quick check-ins to catch any issues early and adjusted our project management software to break his tasks into smaller, more manageable chunks."

Result: "As a result of these changes, the developer's productivity improved significantly. He completed his portion of the project on time, and we successfully launched the software update two days ahead of schedule. Moreover, this experience led to a lasting improvement in team communication and collaboration. In our next project, I noticed team members were more proactive about seeking help when needed, which contributed to a 20% reduction in bug fixes during the testing phase."

Tips for Mastering Behavioral Questions

1. Prepare a diverse set of examples: Before the interview, reflect on your experiences and prepare stories that demonstrate various competencies. Have at least 5-7 robust examples that can be adapted to different questions.

2. Be specific: Use real situations and provide concrete details. Avoid hypotheticals or generalizations.

3. Choose relevant examples: Tailor your stories to the job you're applying for. Review the job description and company values to identify key competencies they're likely to ask about.

4. Practice, but don't memorize: Rehearse your stories using the STAR format, but avoid memorizing them word-for-word. You want to sound natural and be able to adapt your example to the specific question asked.

5. Keep it concise: Aim to keep your responses to 2-3 minutes. Practice trimming unnecessary details while still providing a clear, compelling narrative.

6. Emphasize your role: While it's fine to mention teamwork, make sure you highlight your specific contributions and decision-making process.

7. Quantify results when possible: Numbers and percentages can make your achievements more concrete and impressive.

3. BEHAVIORAL QUESTIONS: PROVING YOUR WORTH WITH THE STAR...

8. Be honest: Don't exaggerate or fabricate stories. Experienced interviewers can often detect insincerity.

9. Reflect on lessons learned: Even if the outcome wasn't perfect, showing what you learned demonstrates growth and self-awareness.

10. Listen carefully to the question: Make sure you're answering exactly what's being asked. It's okay to take a moment to think before you respond.

Common Behavioral Questions to Prepare For

While you can't predict every question, here are some frequently asked behavioral questions:

- Describe a time when you had to meet a tight deadline.
    - Tell me about a situation where you had to resolve a conflict with a coworker.
    - Give an example of a time you showed leadership.
    - Describe a situation where you had to learn a new skill quickly.
    - Tell me about a time you made a mistake and how you handled it.
    - Give an example of how you've contributed to improving a process or procedure.

Conclusion

Mastering behavioral questions through the STAR method can significantly boost your interview performance. This approach allows you to showcase your skills and experiences in a structured, compelling manner. Remember, the key is to prepare thoroughly, practice your delivery, and remain authentic in your responses.

By providing concrete examples of your past successes and learning experiences, you give the interviewer a clear picture of the value you can bring to their organization. With consistent practice and refinement of your STAR responses, you'll approach behavioral questions with confidence, effectively proving your worth to potential employers.

4. Situational and Problem-Solving Questions: Showcasing Your Skills

Situational and problem-solving questions are powerful tools that interviewers use to assess your critical thinking, creativity, and ability to handle real-world challenges. Unlike behavioral questions that focus on past experiences, these questions often present hypothetical scenarios or ask you to solve specific problems on the spot. Mastering these questions can significantly boost your interview performance and demonstrate your potential value to the organization.

Understanding Situational and Problem-Solving Questions

Situational questions typically begin with phrases like:
  - "How would you handle…"
  - "What would you do if…"
  - "Imagine that…"

Problem-solving questions might be more direct:
  - "How would you improve…"
  - "What steps would you take to…"
  - "Can you walk me through how you'd solve…"

These questions aim to evaluate several key competencies:
  - Critical thinking and analytical skills

- Decision-making ability
- Creativity and innovation
- Adaptability and flexibility
- Prioritization and time management
- Leadership and teamwork
- Ethical judgment

Strategies for Tackling Situational and Problem-Solving Questions

1. Understand the Question

Before diving into your answer, make sure you fully understand what's being asked. Don't hesitate to ask for clarification if needed. This shows thoughtfulness and ensures you're addressing the right issue.

2. Structure Your Response

Use a clear structure for your answer. For situational questions, you might adapt the STAR method (Situation, Task, Action, Result) to fit a hypothetical scenario. For problem-solving questions, consider using a step-by-step approach:
   a) Identify the problem
   b) Gather information
   c) Generate possible solutions
   d) Evaluate options
   e) Choose and implement a solution
   f) Review and adjust

3. Think Aloud

Verbalize your thought process. Interviewers are often more interested in how you approach a problem than the specific solution you propose. This demonstrates your analytical skills and problem-solving methodology.

4. Draw from Experience

While the scenario might be hypothetical, you can still draw insights from your past experiences. Mention relevant situations you've encountered or skills you've developed that would help in the given scenario.

5. Consider Multiple Perspectives

Show that you can see the big picture. Consider how your proposed solution might affect different stakeholders or departments within the organization.

6. Demonstrate Flexibility

Acknowledge that there might be multiple valid approaches. Show that you're open to feedback and willing to adjust your strategy if needed.

7. Align with Company Values

If possible, incorporate the company's values or mission into your response. This shows that you've done your research and understand the organization's culture.

8. Quantify When Possible

Even in hypothetical scenarios, try to provide concrete metrics or goals. This demonstrates a results-oriented mindset.

Example Situational Question and Response

Question: "Imagine you're leading a team project and one team member consistently misses deadlines, jeopardizing the project's timeline. How would you handle this situation?"

Response: "I would approach this situation systematically to ensure the project's success while addressing the team member's performance issues. Here's how I'd handle it:

First, I'd gather information to understand the root cause of the missed deadlines. I'd schedule a private one-on-one meeting with the team member to discuss their challenges. It's crucial to approach this conversation with empathy, as there might be personal or professional issues affecting their performance.

Based on this discussion, I'd work with the team member to develop an action plan. This might include breaking tasks into smaller, more manageable chunks, providing additional resources or training if needed, or adjusting their responsibilities to better match their strengths.

I'd also implement more frequent check-ins, perhaps daily or every other day, to monitor progress and provide support. This increased oversight would be framed as a way to help them succeed, not as a punishment.

Simultaneously, I'd review the overall project timeline and workload distribution. I might need to reallocate some tasks to ensure we meet our deadlines. I'd communicate any changes transparently to the entire team, without singling out the struggling team member.

If performance doesn't improve after these interventions, I'd involve HR or upper management to discuss further steps, which might include formal performance improvement plans or considering changes to the team composition.

Throughout this process, I'd document all actions taken and their outcomes. This serves two purposes: it provides a clear record if further action is needed, and it allows us to analyze what strategies were most effective for future reference.

My goal would be to find a solution that keeps the project on track while giving the team member the support they need to improve. By addressing the issue promptly and constructively, we can minimize its impact on the project and potentially turn it into a growth opportunity for the team member and the team as a whole."

4. SITUATIONAL AND PROBLEM-SOLVING QUESTIONS: SHOWCASING...

Example Problem-Solving Question and Response

Question: "Our company is experiencing a 20% customer churn rate. How would you approach reducing this?"

Response: "Reducing customer churn is crucial for sustainable growth. I'd approach this problem methodically:

1. Data Analysis: First, I'd dive deep into the data to understand patterns in customer churn. Are there specific products, services, or time periods associated with higher churn? Are certain customer segments more likely to leave? This analysis would help identify potential root causes.

2. Customer Feedback: I'd implement a robust feedback collection system, including exit surveys for churned customers, to gain qualitative insights into why customers are leaving.

3. Customer Journey Mapping: I'd create detailed customer journey maps to identify pain points or gaps in the customer experience that might be contributing to churn.

4. Competitive Analysis: I'd research our competitors to understand if they're offering something we're not, or if there are industry trends we're not addressing.

5. Develop Hypotheses: Based on the data gathered, I'd formulate hypotheses about the main drivers of churn.

6. Prioritize and Test Solutions: I'd prioritize potential solutions based on expected impact and ease of implementation. These might include:
    - Improving onboarding processes to ensure customers fully understand and utilize our products
    - Implementing a proactive customer success program to identify at-risk

customers early
  - Enhancing our product features or user experience based on customer feedback
  - Developing a loyalty program to incentivize long-term relationships
  - Adjusting pricing or creating more flexible plans if cost is a major factor

7. Implement and Monitor: I'd suggest implementing these solutions in phases, starting with a pilot program if possible. We'd closely monitor the impact of each intervention on the churn rate.

8. Continuous Improvement: Based on the results, we'd refine our approach, scaling successful initiatives and adjusting or discarding less effective ones.

9. Long-term Strategy: Finally, I'd recommend incorporating churn reduction into our overall business strategy, including regular reviews and setting specific retention targets.

By taking this comprehensive, data-driven approach, I believe we could significantly reduce the churn rate. Even a 5% reduction in churn could have a substantial impact on our bottom line and long-term growth prospects."

Conclusion

Mastering situational and problem-solving questions requires practice and preparation. By developing a structured approach to these questions, you can showcase your analytical skills, creativity, and ability to handle complex challenges. Remember to stay calm, think logically, and communicate your thought process clearly. These questions are your opportunity to demonstrate how you'd add value to the organization by effectively navigating real-world business scenarios.

5. Technical and Industry-Specific Questions: Demonstrating Expertise

Technical and industry-specific questions are designed to assess your specialized knowledge and skills directly related to the job you're applying for. These questions can vary widely depending on your field, from coding challenges for software developers to case studies for consultants, or specific regulatory knowledge for finance professionals. Excelling in this area of the interview can set you apart as a top candidate and demonstrate your readiness to contribute immediately to the role.

Preparing for Technical Questions

1. Review the Job Description
Start by thoroughly analyzing the job description. Highlight technical skills, tools, and industry knowledge mentioned. These are likely areas the interviewer will focus on.

2. Brush Up on Fundamentals
Regardless of your experience level, review the fundamental concepts in your field. Interviewers often test basic knowledge to ensure you have a solid foundation.

3. Stay Current
Industries evolve rapidly. Stay informed about recent developments,

emerging technologies, and current trends in your field. This demonstrates your commitment to professional growth.

4. Practice Technical Explanations

Work on explaining complex concepts in simple terms. This skill is valuable not just for the interview but also for collaborating with non-technical team members.

5. Prepare for Hands-On Tests

Many technical interviews include practical tests or coding challenges. Practice these skills regularly leading up to your interview.

Types of Technical and Industry-Specific Questions

1. Knowledge-Based Questions

These straightforward questions test your understanding of key concepts, terminologies, or processes specific to your field.

Example (for a data analyst): "Can you explain the difference between supervised and unsupervised learning in machine learning?"

Strategy: Provide a clear, concise definition of each term and offer a brief example to demonstrate deeper understanding.

2. Scenario-Based Questions

These questions present a hypothetical situation you might encounter on the job and ask how you would handle it.

Example (for a project manager): "How would you approach a project that's fallen behind schedule and is over budget?"

Strategy: Outline a step-by-step approach, demonstrating your problem-solving skills and industry best practices.

5. TECHNICAL AND INDUSTRY-SPECIFIC QUESTIONS: DEMONSTRATING...

3. Tool and Technology Questions

These assess your familiarity with specific software, programming languages, or equipment relevant to the role.

Example (for a graphic designer): "What's your experience with Adobe Creative Suite? Which tools do you use most frequently?"

Strategy: Be honest about your level of proficiency. If you're not familiar with a tool, express your willingness and ability to learn quickly.

4. Case Studies or Problem-Solving Exercises

These are in-depth scenarios that require you to analyze a complex situation and propose solutions.

Example (for a marketing professional): "Our company is launching a new product. Outline a marketing strategy to reach our target demographic of urban professionals aged 25-40."

Strategy: Ask clarifying questions if needed, then structure your response methodically. Explain your reasoning at each step.

5. Coding Challenges (for tech roles)

These involve writing, analyzing, or debugging code during the interview.

Example: "Write a function that determines if a given string is a palindrome."

Strategy: Think aloud as you work through the problem. This gives the interviewer insight into your problem-solving process.

6. Regulatory and Compliance Questions

These are common in fields like finance, healthcare, or law, testing your knowledge of relevant laws and regulations.

Example (for a compliance officer): "What are the key components of an effective anti-money laundering (AML) program?"

Strategy: Clearly outline the main elements, referencing specific regulations where applicable.

7. Industry Trend Analysis

These questions assess your awareness of current developments in your field.

Example (for a renewable energy engineer): "What do you think are the most promising emerging technologies in sustainable energy?"

Strategy: Discuss 2-3 trending technologies, explaining their potential impact and any challenges to their implementation.

Strategies for Excelling in Technical Interviews

1. Use the STAR Method for Scenario Questions

Even in technical interviews, the STAR (Situation, Task, Action, Result) method can be effective for structuring your responses to scenario-based questions.

2. Show Your Work

For problem-solving or coding questions, explain your thought process as you work through the solution. This demonstrates your analytical skills and allows the interviewer to provide guidance if needed.

3. Relate to Past Experiences

Whenever possible, connect your answers to relevant experiences from your past work or projects. This adds credibility to your responses.

4. Be Honest About What You Don't Know

5. TECHNICAL AND INDUSTRY-SPECIFIC QUESTIONS: DEMONSTRATING...

If you're unsure about a question, it's better to admit it than to try to bluff. Express your willingness to learn and describe how you would go about finding the answer.

5. Ask Clarifying Questions
Don't hesitate to ask for more information if a question is ambiguous. This shows thoughtfulness and ensures you're addressing the right issue.

6. Demonstrate Continuous Learning
Highlight any recent courses, certifications, or self-study you've undertaken. This shows your commitment to staying current in your field.

7. Use Industry Jargon Appropriately
While it's important to demonstrate your knowledge of industry-specific terms, make sure you're using them correctly and not overdoing it.

8. Prepare Relevant Examples
Have a few examples ready of projects you've worked on or challenges you've overcome that showcase your technical skills.

9. Show Enthusiasm
Demonstrate genuine interest in the technical aspects of the role. Enthusiasm for your field can be as important as knowledge.

10. Practice Active Listening
Pay close attention to the details of each question. Technical interviewers often include important information in the way they phrase questions.

Example Technical Interview Exchange

Interviewer: "We're considering migrating our on-premises database to a cloud solution. What factors would you consider in making this decision, and how would you approach the migration process?"

Candidate: "This is an important decision that can significantly impact the company's operations and data management. Here's how I would approach it:

Factors to consider:

1. Cost: Comparing long-term costs of on-premises vs. cloud solutions, including hardware, maintenance, and scalability.
2. Performance: Assessing potential impact on data access speed and application performance.
3. Security: Evaluating the security measures offered by cloud providers compared to our current setup.
4. Compliance: Ensuring the cloud solution meets any regulatory requirements for data storage and handling.
5. Scalability: Considering future growth and the ease of scaling in a cloud environment.
6. Downtime: Planning for potential disruptions during the migration process.

Migration approach:

1. Assessment: Thoroughly analyze the current database structure, dependencies, and usage patterns.
2. Planning: Develop a detailed migration plan, including timelines, resource allocation, and risk mitigation strategies.
3. Choose the right cloud solution: Based on our needs, select the most appropriate cloud provider and service (e.g., AWS RDS, Azure SQL Database).
4. Data preparation: Clean and optimize the current database for migration.
5. Testing: Set up a test environment to validate the migration process and identify any issues.

6. Migration: Perform the actual migration, potentially using a phased approach to minimize disruption.
7. Validation: Thoroughly test the new cloud-based system to ensure data integrity and performance.
8. Optimization: Fine-tune the cloud database for optimal performance.
9. Training: Provide necessary training for the team on managing and using the new cloud-based system.
10. Monitoring: Implement robust monitoring to track performance and costs in the new environment.

In my previous role, I led a similar migration project where we moved a 5TB database to AWS RDS. We encountered challenges with data transfer speeds, which we resolved by using AWS Snowball for the initial bulk data transfer. This experience taught me the importance of thorough planning and testing in such migrations."

Conclusion

Mastering technical and industry-specific questions requires a combination of deep knowledge, problem-solving skills, and the ability to communicate complex ideas clearly. By thoroughly preparing and practicing your responses, you can confidently showcase your expertise and demonstrate your value to potential employers. Remember, these questions are not just tests of your knowledge, but opportunities to show how you apply that knowledge to real-world scenarios.

6. Leadership and Management Questions: For Career Advancement

Leadership and management questions are crucial components of interviews for senior positions or roles with growth potential. These questions aim to assess your ability to guide teams, make strategic decisions, and drive organizational success. Even if you're not applying for a management position, demonstrating leadership qualities can set you apart as a candidate with high potential for future advancement.

Understanding Leadership and Management Questions

These questions typically focus on several key areas:

1. Vision and Strategy
2. Team Management and Development
3. Decision Making and Problem Solving
4. Communication and Interpersonal Skills
5. Change Management
6. Conflict Resolution
7. Performance Management
8. Ethical Leadership

6. LEADERSHIP AND MANAGEMENT QUESTIONS: FOR CAREER...

Preparing for Leadership and Management Questions

1. Reflect on Your Experience
   Even if you haven't held a formal leadership role, consider situations where you've taken initiative, led projects, or influenced others.

2. Develop a Leadership Philosophy
   Articulate your approach to leadership. What are your core values? How do you inspire and motivate others?

3. Stay Informed on Leadership Trends
   Familiarize yourself with current leadership theories and best practices in management.

4. Prepare Specific Examples
   Use the STAR method (Situation, Task, Action, Result) to structure stories that demonstrate your leadership skills.

Common Leadership and Management Questions and Strategies to Answer Them

1. "What's your leadership style?"

Strategy: Describe your approach to leadership, emphasizing flexibility and adaptability. Provide an example of how you've successfully applied this style.

Example Answer: "I believe in a situational leadership approach, adapting my style based on the team's needs and the specific challenges at hand. Generally, I lean towards a collaborative style that empowers team members to contribute their ideas and take ownership of their work.

For instance, when leading a cross-functional team on a new product launch,

I recognized that team members had varying levels of experience. I provided more direct guidance to less experienced members while giving more autonomy to seasoned professionals. This approach fostered a supportive environment where everyone could contribute effectively. As a result, we launched the product two weeks ahead of schedule and exceeded our first-quarter sales targets by 20%."

2. "How do you motivate your team?"

Strategy: Discuss your understanding of intrinsic and extrinsic motivation. Emphasize your ability to recognize individual needs and align them with organizational goals.

Example Answer: "I believe motivation stems from a combination of personal growth, recognition, and alignment with meaningful goals. My approach involves:

1. Understanding individual aspirations: I have regular one-on-ones to discuss career goals and personal development.
2. Providing challenging opportunities: I assign stretch projects that push team members to grow.
3. Recognizing achievements: I ensure both public recognition and personal acknowledgment of good work.
4. Fostering a positive work environment: I promote open communication and celebrate team successes.
5. Connecting daily tasks to larger goals: I help team members see how their work contributes to the company's mission.

In my previous role, I implemented a peer recognition program that boosted team morale and increased productivity by 15% over six months."

3. "Describe a time when you had to make a difficult decision as a leader."

Strategy: Choose an example that showcases your analytical skills, ethical judgment, and ability to handle the consequences of your decisions.

Example Answer: "In my role as a project manager, I faced a critical decision when our key software developer unexpectedly left mid-project. We were already on a tight deadline for a major client.

I had to choose between pushing the remaining team to work overtime to meet the deadline or informing the client that we needed to extend the timeline. I gathered data on the team's current workload, the project's critical path, and the potential impact on team morale and project quality.

After careful consideration, I decided to have an honest conversation with the client about extending the deadline. I presented a revised plan that included bringing on a contract developer to support the team.

Initially, the client was disappointed, but they appreciated our transparency and comprehensive solution. This decision maintained team morale, ensured project quality, and ultimately strengthened our relationship with the client. They've since engaged us for three additional projects."

4. "How do you handle conflict within your team?"

Strategy: Emphasize your ability to address conflicts promptly and constructively. Highlight your communication skills and focus on finding win-win solutions.

Example Answer: "I view conflict as an opportunity for growth and improvement when managed properly. My approach to conflict resolution involves:

1. Active listening: I ensure all parties feel heard and understood.
2. Identifying the root cause: I look beyond the surface issue to understand underlying factors.
3. Facilitating open dialogue: I create a safe space for team members to express their concerns.
4. Focusing on common goals: I remind the team of our shared objectives.
5. Collaborative problem-solving: I involve all parties in generating solutions.

For example, I once mediated a conflict between our marketing and product teams over project priorities. By facilitating a structured discussion, we uncovered that the real issue was a lack of clear communication channels. We implemented a new project management tool and regular cross-team meetings, which not only resolved the immediate conflict but improved overall collaboration."

5. "How do you approach change management?"

Strategy: Demonstrate your understanding of the challenges inherent in change and your ability to lead people through transitions.

Example Answer: "Effective change management is crucial for organizational growth and adaptation. My approach involves:

1. Clear communication: I articulate the reasons for change and the expected benefits.
2. Stakeholder involvement: I identify key stakeholders and involve them in the planning process.
3. Addressing concerns: I proactively address fears and resistance through open dialogue.
4. Phased implementation: I break down large changes into manageable

steps.
5. Continuous feedback: I establish channels for ongoing feedback and adjust plans as needed.
6. Celebrating milestones: I recognize progress to maintain momentum.

When our company transitioned to a new CRM system, I led the change management process. By involving end-users in the selection and customization process, providing comprehensive training, and addressing concerns promptly, we achieved a 95% adoption rate within three months, significantly higher than industry averages for similar transitions."

6. "How do you develop your team members?"

Strategy: Highlight your commitment to continuous learning and your ability to identify and nurture talent.

Example Answer: "I believe in creating a culture of continuous learning and growth. My approach to team development includes:

1. Regular skill assessments: I work with team members to identify areas for improvement and growth opportunities.
2. Personalized development plans: I collaborate with each team member to create tailored learning objectives.
3. Mentoring and coaching: I provide ongoing guidance and support.
4. Cross-training opportunities: I encourage team members to learn skills outside their primary roles.
5. Stretch assignments: I delegate challenging tasks to push team members out of their comfort zones.
6. Learning resources: I ensure access to relevant training, workshops, and educational materials.

In my last role, I implemented a 'skill-share' program where team members taught each other new skills. This not only facilitated learning but also improved team cohesion and communication. As a result, we saw a 30% increase in internal promotions over two years."

Conclusion

Leadership and management questions provide an opportunity to showcase your ability to guide, inspire, and develop others while driving organizational success. By preparing thoughtful responses that highlight your experience, skills, and leadership philosophy, you can demonstrate your readiness for career advancement.

Remember, effective leadership is not just about having the right answers, but about asking the right questions, listening actively, and fostering an environment where others can excel. As you prepare for these questions, focus on how you've positively impacted others and contributed to organizational goals. Your responses should reflect not only your past achievements but also your potential to take on greater responsibilities in the future.

7. Curve ball Questions: Handling the Unexpected with Confidence

Curve ball questions, also known as oddball or off-the-wall questions, are designed to catch you off guard and assess how you think on your feet. These questions may seem irrelevant or even bizarre, but they serve several purposes:

1. Testing your creativity and problem-solving skills
2. Evaluating your ability to handle unexpected situations
3. Assessing your personality and cultural fit
4. Observing how you perform under pressure

While it's impossible to predict every curveball question, understanding their purpose and having a strategy to approach them can help you navigate these challenging interview moments with confidence.

Types of Curveball Questions

1. Abstract Reasoning Questions
    Example: "How many tennis balls can you fit in a limousine?"

2. Personal Preference Questions

Example: "If you were a superhero, what would your superpower be?"

3. Ethical Dilemmas
Example: "Is it ever okay to lie in business?"

4. Hypothetical Scenarios
Example: "If you were shrunk to the size of a pencil and put in a blender, how would you get out?"

5. Brainteasers
Example: "Why are manhole covers round?"

6. Open-ended Questions
Example: "Tell me something that's true, that almost nobody agrees with you on."

Strategies for Handling Curveball Questions

1. Stay Calm and Composed
The first step in handling a curveball question is to remain calm. Take a deep breath and remember that the interviewer is more interested in your thought process than in a "correct" answer.

2. Take Your Time
It's okay to pause briefly to gather your thoughts. You can say something like, "That's an interesting question. Let me think about that for a moment."

3. Ask for Clarification if Needed
If the question is unclear, don't hesitate to ask for more information. This shows that you're thoughtful and want to provide a relevant answer.

4. Think Out Loud
Share your thought process with the interviewer. This gives them insight

into how you approach problems and make decisions.

5. Be Creative and Playful
Curveball questions often invite creative thinking. Don't be afraid to think outside the box and even inject a bit of humor if appropriate.

6. Relate Your Answer Back to the Job
If possible, try to connect your response to skills or qualities relevant to the position you're applying for.

7. Be Honest
If the question asks for a personal opinion, be genuine in your response. There's often no right or wrong answer; the interviewer is looking for authenticity and self-awareness.

8. Use Logic and Structure
For questions that require problem-solving, use a logical approach. Break down the problem into smaller parts if necessary.

Example Curveball Questions and Responses

1. Question: "How would you solve problems if you were from Mars?"

Strategy: This question tests your creativity and ability to think abstractly. Use it as an opportunity to showcase your problem-solving approach.

Response: "That's an intriguing question. As a Martian, I'd likely have a completely different perspective on Earth's problems. I'd start by observing and gathering data to understand the context of Earth's challenges, much like I've done in preparing for this interview by researching your company.

Then, I'd leverage my unique Martian viewpoint to propose innovative solutions that Earthlings might not have considered. This could involve using advanced Martian technology or applying principles from Martian society that have proven successful.

However, I'd also recognize that my outsider perspective might miss crucial cultural or historical context. So, I'd collaborate with Earth experts, combining my fresh ideas with their deep understanding of local issues. This approach of blending diverse perspectives to drive innovation is something I've always valued in my work, whether on Earth or Mars."

2. Question: "If you were a kitchen appliance, which one would you be and why?"

Strategy: This type of question assesses your self-awareness and ability to draw creative parallels. Use it to highlight qualities that are relevant to the job.

Response: "I'd say I'm most like a food processor. Like a food processor, I'm versatile and can handle a variety of tasks efficiently. I can quickly break down complex problems into manageable pieces, much like a food processor breaks down ingredients.

I'm also adaptable – just as a food processor can switch between slicing, dicing, and pureeing, I can adjust my approach based on the needs of the project or team.

Moreover, I'm a facilitator. A food processor doesn't create the recipe, but it makes executing the recipe much easier and more efficient. Similarly, in my work, I excel at taking ideas and plans and turning them into reality, streamlining processes to achieve the best results.

Lastly, like a reliable food processor, I'm consistent and dependable. You can count on me to deliver quality work, time after time."

3. Question: "Sell me this pen."

Strategy: This classic sales question tests your ability to think on your feet and demonstrate persuasive skills. Use a consultative selling approach.

Response: "Before I try to sell you this pen, I'd like to ask you a few questions if that's okay. What do you typically use pens for in your daily work? Are there any frustrations you have with your current pens?

[Interviewer responds]

I see. Based on what you've told me, this pen could be an excellent solution for you. Its ergonomic design addresses your concern about hand fatigue during long writing sessions. The quick-drying ink would be perfect for your left-handed writing style, preventing smudges on your important documents.

Moreover, given your role in signing crucial contracts, the pen's professional appearance and smooth writing experience could subtly enhance your image of attention to detail and quality.

Considering the amount of time you spend writing and the importance of the documents you work with, investing in a high-quality pen like this one isn't just a purchase – it's an investment in your productivity and professional image. Would you like to give it a try?"

4. Question: "How many bricks would it take to build a replica of the Empire State Building?"

Strategy: This estimation question tests your problem-solving skills and ability to make reasonable assumptions. Break down the problem and think aloud.

Response: "To approach this problem, I'd need to make several assumptions and break it down into steps:

1. Estimate the dimensions of the Empire State Building. Let's say it's roughly 400 meters tall, 60 meters wide, and 60 meters deep.

2. Calculate the volume: 400 x 60 x 60 = 1,440,000 cubic meters.

3. Estimate the size of a standard brick. Let's say 0.2m x 0.1m x 0.06m = 0.0012 cubic meters.

4. Divide the building volume by the brick volume: 1,440,000 / 0.0012 = 1,200,000,000 bricks.

5. Account for windows, interior spaces, and non-brick materials. Let's reduce our estimate by 25%.

Final estimate: About 900,000,000 bricks.

Of course, this is a rough estimation. In a real project, we'd need precise measurements and would likely use computer modeling for accuracy. This approach of breaking down complex problems, making reasonable assumptions, and showing my work process is how I tackle challenges in my professional work as well."

Conclusion

Curveball questions can be challenging, but they also present an opportunity to showcase your creativity, problem-solving skills, and ability to perform under pressure. Remember, there's often no "right" answer to these questions. Interviewers are more interested in your thought process, creativity, and how you handle unexpected situations.

When faced with a curveball question:

7. CURVE BALL QUESTIONS: HANDLING THE UNEXPECTED WITH...

1. Stay calm and composed
2. Take time to think if needed
3. Ask for clarification if the question is unclear
4. Share your thought process
5. Be creative and, if appropriate, inject some humor
6. Try to relate your answer back to the job or your skills
7. Be honest and authentic in your responses
8. Use logic and structure in your approach

By following these strategies and practicing your responses to various types of unexpected questions, you can turn these challenging moments into opportunities to impress your interviewer and stand out as a confident, creative, and adaptable candidate.

8. Questions for Career Changers and Fresh Graduates

Career changers and fresh graduates often face unique challenges in job interviews. Employers may have concerns about their lack of direct experience or how well they'll adapt to a new field. However, with the right preparation, these candidates can turn their diverse backgrounds or fresh perspectives into strengths. This chapter will cover common questions for career changers and fresh graduates, along with strategies for crafting compelling responses.

Questions for Career Changers

1. "Why are you changing careers?"

Strategy: Be honest about your motivations while emphasizing your enthusiasm for the new field. Connect your past experiences to your new career goals.

Example Answer: "After five years in marketing, I realized my favorite part of the job was analyzing campaign data. This sparked my interest in data science. I've always been drawn to solving complex problems, and I see data science as a field where I can apply my analytical skills to drive business decisions. My marketing background gives me a unique perspective on how data insights can be applied practically in business contexts. I've been preparing for this

8. QUESTIONS FOR CAREER CHANGERS AND FRESH GRADUATES

transition by completing an online data science bootcamp and working on several personal projects, which have only reinforced my passion for this field."

2. "How do your previous experiences relate to this new field?"

Strategy: Identify transferable skills and experiences that are relevant to the new role. Focus on core competencies rather than specific technical skills.

Example Answer: "While healthcare technology might seem far from my previous role in financial services, there are significant overlaps in the core skills required. In finance, I developed strong analytical abilities, attention to detail, and experience in managing sensitive data – all crucial in healthcare tech. My experience in regulatory compliance in finance translates well to the heavily regulated healthcare industry. Moreover, my client-facing roles have honed my communication skills, which are essential when explaining complex technical concepts to healthcare professionals. I'm excited to apply these skills in a new context where I can make a direct impact on patient care."

3. "Are you prepared for a potential pay cut or step back in seniority?"

Strategy: Show that you've carefully considered the implications of your career change and that you're focused on long-term growth.

Example Answer: "I've given this a lot of thought, and I'm prepared for the possibility of a pay adjustment or change in seniority. My priority is gaining experience in this new field and building a foundation for long-term career growth. I've planned financially for this transition, and I'm confident that the skills and experience I'll gain will be invaluable. I see this as an investment in my future, and I'm excited about the potential for growth and advancement as I prove myself in this new role."

4. "How will you get up to speed in this new field?"

Strategy: Highlight any preparation you've already done and your plan for continued learning.

Example Answer: "I've been proactively preparing for this transition. I've completed several relevant online courses, including [specific courses]. I'm also an active member of [relevant professional organization], which has allowed me to network with industry professionals and stay current on trends. I'm a quick learner, and I plan to take advantage of any training opportunities offered by the company. Additionally, I've identified several key industry publications and podcasts that I follow regularly. I'm committed to continuous learning and am excited to immerse myself in this new field."

Questions for Fresh Graduates

1. "How has your education prepared you for this role?"

Strategy: Connect specific aspects of your education to job requirements. Highlight relevant projects, internships, or coursework.

Example Answer: "My degree in Computer Science has given me a strong foundation in software development principles and practices. Particularly relevant to this role, I completed advanced courses in machine learning and data structures. For my final year project, I developed a predictive analytics tool for a local business, which allowed me to apply my skills to a real-world problem. This experience not only enhanced my technical skills but also taught me how to communicate complex technical concepts to non-technical stakeholders – a skill I understand is valuable in this role."

2. "What experience do you have that's relevant to this position?"

Strategy: Don't limit yourself to paid work experience. Consider internships,

8. QUESTIONS FOR CAREER CHANGERS AND FRESH GRADUATES

volunteer work, academic projects, and extracurricular activities.

Example Answer: "While I'm a recent graduate, I've actively sought experiences that align with this role. During my internship at XYZ Corp, I was part of a team that developed a new customer relationship management system, which improved client retention rates by 15%. I also led a student project to create a mobile app for campus event management, which required me to coordinate a team of five and manage the entire project lifecycle. Additionally, as the treasurer of our university's entrepreneurship club, I gained valuable experience in budgeting and financial reporting. These experiences have honed my technical skills, project management abilities, and teamwork – all of which are crucial for this position."

3. "How do you plan to transition from academic life to a professional environment?"

Strategy: Demonstrate your awareness of the differences between academic and professional settings, and your readiness to adapt.

Example Answer: "I understand that the transition from university to a professional environment involves some adjustments, and I'm prepared for that. In my final year, I intentionally structured my schedule to mirror a typical workday, which helped me develop strong time management skills. I've also gained professional experience through my internship at ABC Company, where I learned to navigate office dynamics and professional communication. I'm a quick learner and am excited to immerse myself in your company culture. I plan to observe and learn from my colleagues, seek feedback regularly, and continuously improve my professional skills."

4. "Where do you see yourself in five years?"

Strategy: Show ambition and a desire for growth, but also a commitment to the role and company you're applying to.

Example Answer: "In five years, I hope to have grown into a role with more responsibilities, perhaps leading a small team or managing key projects. I'm particularly interested in the intersection of technology and sustainability, which aligns well with your company's mission. I plan to continue expanding my technical skills, possibly pursuing relevant certifications in project management or specialized areas of software development. Ultimately, I aim to be in a position where I can contribute significantly to the company's innovation efforts while mentoring newer team members."

General Strategies for Career Changers and Fresh Graduates

1. Emphasize Transferable Skills
Both career changers and fresh graduates should focus on core competencies that transfer across roles and industries, such as communication, problem-solving, adaptability, and teamwork.

2. Showcase Your Unique Perspective
Career changers can highlight how their diverse background brings a fresh perspective to the role. Fresh graduates can emphasize their up-to-date knowledge of the latest industry trends and technologies.

3. Demonstrate Enthusiasm and Willingness to Learn
Show that you're excited about the opportunity and committed to continuous learning and growth.

4. Provide Concrete Examples
Whenever possible, support your answers with specific examples from your experiences, no matter how limited they might seem.

5. Address Potential Concerns Proactively
Anticipate and address any concerns the employer might have about your lack of direct experience or industry knowledge.

6. Highlight Relevant Projects or Self-Study

Discuss any personal projects, volunteer work, or self-study you've undertaken to prepare for this career move or to supplement your formal education.

7. Network and Seek Mentorship

Mention any industry professionals you've connected with or any mentorship relationships you've developed. This shows initiative and a commitment to professional growth.

8. Be Honest About Your Learning Curve

It's okay to acknowledge areas where you'll need to grow. Pair this with a clear plan for how you intend to acquire the necessary skills and knowledge.

Conclusion

For career changers and fresh graduates, job interviews are an opportunity to showcase your unique value proposition. While you may lack traditional experience, you bring fresh perspectives, transferable skills, and a strong motivation to learn and grow. By preparing thoughtful responses to these common questions and following the strategies outlined, you can effectively communicate your potential and convince employers that you're the right fit for the role.

Remember, every experienced professional was once a newcomer to their field. Your enthusiasm, adaptability, and fresh perspective can be significant assets to an employer. By framing your responses positively and demonstrating your commitment to growth and learning, you can turn your status as a career changer or fresh graduate from a potential weakness into a compelling strength.

9. Crafting Memorable Answers: Tailoring Your Responses

Crafting memorable answers is an essential skill that can set you apart from other candidates in a job interview. It's not just about providing correct information; it's about presenting your experiences, skills, and personality in a way that resonates with the interviewer and aligns with the company's needs. This chapter will explore strategies for tailoring your responses to make a lasting impression.

Understanding the Importance of Tailored Responses

Generic answers rarely impress interviewers. They've likely heard similar responses many times before. Tailoring your answers shows that:

1. You've done your research on the company and role
2. You're genuinely interested in the position
3. You can connect your experiences to the job requirements
4. You're thoughtful and prepared

Key Elements of Memorable Answers

9. CRAFTING MEMORABLE ANSWERS: TAILORING YOUR RESPONSES

1. Relevance: Directly address the question and relate it to the job.
2. Specificity: Use concrete examples and details.
3. Structure: Organize your thoughts clearly and logically.
4. Brevity: Be concise while providing sufficient detail.
5. Authenticity: Show your personality and genuine enthusiasm.

Strategies for Tailoring Your Responses

1. Research Thoroughly

Before the interview, dive deep into:
   - The company's mission, values, and culture
   - Recent news or developments about the company
   - The specific role and its requirements
   - Industry trends and challenges

Use this information to frame your answers in a context that's relevant to the company and position.

2. Use the STAR Method Effectively

The STAR (Situation, Task, Action, Result) method is a powerful tool for structuring your responses, especially for behavioral questions. Here's how to tailor it:

Situation: Choose a scenario that's relevant to the role you're applying for.
   Task: Highlight responsibilities that align with the job requirements.
   Action: Focus on actions that demonstrate skills the company values.
   Result: Quantify your achievements and relate them to the company's goals.

Example:

Question: "Tell me about a time you led a team through a difficult project."

Tailored STAR Response: "In my previous role at XYZ Corp, we faced a challenge similar to what I understand your company is currently experiencing with rapid market changes (Situation). As the project lead, I was tasked with redesigning our main product to meet new customer demands while keeping within a tight budget and timeline (Task). I implemented an agile development process, which I see your company also values, and held daily stand-ups to ensure clear communication and quick problem-solving (Action). As a result, we launched the redesigned product two weeks ahead of schedule, and it led to a 25% increase in customer satisfaction scores (Result). I'm excited about the possibility of bringing this experience and approach to the challenges your team is facing."

3. Mirror the Company's Language

Pay attention to the language used in the job description and company materials. Incorporate key terms and phrases into your responses to demonstrate cultural fit.

4. Prepare Adaptable Anecdotes

Develop a repertoire of professional stories that can be adapted to various questions. For each story, consider multiple angles that could be emphasized depending on the specific question asked.

5. Address the Underlying Question

Often, interview questions have layers. Consider what the interviewer is really trying to assess and address that in your response.

Example:
  Surface Question: "What's your greatest weakness?"

9. CRAFTING MEMORABLE ANSWERS: TAILORING YOUR RESPONSES

Underlying Assessment: Can you self-reflect? Are you proactive about self-improvement?

Tailored Response: "I've found that I sometimes focus too much on details, which can impact my efficiency. However, I've recognized this and have been actively working on it. I've implemented a personal kanban board to prioritize tasks and set time limits for each phase of a project. In my last role, this helped me improve my productivity by 20% while maintaining the quality of my work. I'm always looking for new strategies to balance thoroughness with efficiency, which I believe is crucial in a fast-paced environment like yours."

6. Use the CAR Technique for Technical Questions

For technical or role-specific questions, use the Challenge, Action, Result (CAR) technique:

Challenge: Briefly describe a relevant technical problem.
　Action: Explain your approach and the tools/methods you used.
　Result: Share the outcome and any lessons learned.

This structure helps you showcase your technical skills while demonstrating problem-solving abilities.

7. Incorporate Company Research

Weave your knowledge of the company into your answers to show genuine interest and preparation.

Example:
　Question: "Why do you want to work here?"

Tailored Response: "I'm impressed by your company's commitment to sustainability, particularly your recent initiative to reduce carbon emissions by 50% over the next five years. This aligns perfectly with my background in environmental engineering and my passion for creating eco-friendly solutions. I'm excited about the possibility of contributing to this goal, perhaps by applying my experience in optimizing energy consumption in manufacturing processes, which led to a 30% reduction in energy use in my previous role."

8. Customize Your Strengths and Weaknesses

When discussing strengths, focus on those most relevant to the role. For weaknesses, choose ones that aren't critical to the job and emphasize your improvement efforts.

9. Use Power Words

Incorporate impactful words that align with the company's values and the role's requirements. Words like "initiated," "transformed," "streamlined," or "pioneered" can make your answers more dynamic.

10. Practice Active Listening

During the interview, pay close attention to the interviewer's questions and comments. Use this information to further tailor your responses as the interview progresses.

11. Prepare for Follow-up Questions

Anticipate potential follow-up questions to your prepared answers. This allows you to dive deeper and provide more tailored information if asked.

12. Use the "Sandwich Technique" for Negative Experiences

9. CRAFTING MEMORABLE ANSWERS: TAILORING YOUR RESPONSES

When discussing challenges or failures, use this structure:
- Positive: Start with a positive framing
- Negative: Briefly mention the challenge
- Positive: Focus on lessons learned and positive outcomes

Example:
Question: "Tell me about a time you failed."

Tailored Response: "I believe that challenges are opportunities for growth. In my previous role, we missed a critical deadline for a client project (Negative). However, this experience taught me the importance of setting realistic milestones and improving communication with stakeholders (Positive). I implemented a new project management system that increased our on-time delivery rate by 40% (Positive). I'm eager to bring this proactive approach to problem-solving to your team."

13. Relate Personal Qualities to Company Values

Connect your personal qualities and work style to the company's stated values or culture.

Example:
"I noticed that innovation is a key value for your company. This resonates with me deeply. In my last role, I initiated a 'creativity hour' where team members could brainstorm unconventional solutions to ongoing challenges. This led to the development of a new product feature that increased user engagement by 35%."

Conclusion

Crafting memorable, tailored responses requires preparation, self-reflection, and a deep understanding of the company and role you're applying for. By using these strategies, you can transform standard interview answers into compelling narratives that showcase your unique value proposition. Remember, the goal is not just to answer questions, but to engage in a meaningful dialogue that demonstrates why you're the ideal candidate for the position. With practice and thoughtful preparation, you can create responses that not only answer the interviewer's questions but also leave a lasting, positive impression.

10. Turning Weaknesses into Strengths: The Art of Positive Framing

The dreaded "What is your greatest weakness?" question is a staple of job interviews. While it can be challenging to discuss your shortcomings, mastering the art of positive framing can turn this potential pitfall into an opportunity to showcase your self-awareness, growth mindset, and problem-solving skills. This chapter will explore strategies for addressing weaknesses in a way that ultimately highlights your strengths.

Understanding the Purpose of the Weakness Question

Interviewers ask about weaknesses for several reasons:

1. To assess your self-awareness
2. To understand how you handle challenges
3. To evaluate your commitment to personal growth
4. To gauge your honesty and authenticity

The key is to address these underlying concerns while presenting yourself in the best possible light.

The Positive Framing Approach

Positive framing is not about denying weaknesses or presenting false modesty. Instead, it's a technique that:

1. Acknowledges a genuine area for improvement
2. Demonstrates proactive steps taken to address it
3. Highlights the progress made or lessons learned
4. Shows how this growth process has ultimately become a strength

Steps to Effectively Frame Weaknesses Positively

1. Choose an Authentic Weakness

Select a real weakness, but one that:
  - Is not central to the job requirements
  - You have actively worked on improving
  - Has a silver lining or associated strength

Examples:
  - Public speaking anxiety
  - Difficulty delegating tasks
  - Impatience with long-term projects
  - Overly critical of own work

2. Acknowledge the Weakness Briefly

Start by clearly stating the weakness. Be concise and avoid dwelling on negative aspects.

Example: "In the past, I've struggled with public speaking anxiety."

3. Provide Context

10. TURNING WEAKNESSES INTO STRENGTHS: THE ART OF POSITIVE...

Explain briefly how this weakness has manifested in your professional life.

Example: "This meant I often hesitated to contribute ideas in large meetings or volunteer for presentations."

4. Describe Your Improvement efforts

Detail the specific steps you've taken to address the weakness. This demonstrates self-improvement and problem-solving skills.

Example: "Recognizing the importance of public speaking in my career, I decided to tackle this head-on. I joined a local Toastmasters club and committed to giving a speech at least once a month. I also took an online course on presentation skills and started volunteering to lead team meetings at work."

5. Highlight Progress and Lessons Learned

Share the improvements you've made and any insights gained through the process.

Example: "Over the past year, I've seen significant improvement in my comfort level with public speaking. I've learned techniques to manage anxiety, structure compelling presentations, and engage audiences effectively. Recently, I even volunteered to present our team's quarterly results to the entire department."

6. Connect to a Strength or Positive Outcome

Show how working on this weakness has led to a new strength or beneficial outcome.

Example: "This journey has not only improved my public speaking skills but has also enhanced my overall communication abilities. I'm now more effective in one-on-one client interactions, and I've found that the storytelling techniques I've learned are valuable in written reports as well. My efforts to improve in this area have actually made me a more well-rounded communicator."

7. Relate to the Job or Company

If possible, connect your growth in this area to the requirements of the position or the company's values.

Example: "I understand that client presentations are a key part of this role, and I'm excited to bring my newly developed skills and continuously improving abilities to these important interactions."

Examples of Positively Framed Weaknesses

1. Perfectionism

Weak framing: "I'm a perfectionist, which sometimes makes me slow."
   Strong framing: "I have high standards for my work, which in the past led me to spend too much time perfecting minor details. I've learned to better prioritize tasks and focus my attention on the most impactful aspects of a project. This has allowed me to maintain quality while improving efficiency. In my last role, this balanced approach helped me complete projects 20% faster without sacrificing quality."

2. Difficulty Saying No

Weak framing: "I have trouble saying no, so I often take on too much."
   Strong framing: "I'm naturally eager to help and contribute, which sometimes led me to overcommit. I've learned to better assess my capacity and the strategic value of different tasks. Now, I use this eagerness more

effectively by proactively offering assistance on high-priority projects. This has allowed me to make meaningful contributions while maintaining a manageable workload. My team lead recently commended me for my improved ability to balance multiple priorities effectively."

3. Lack of Experience with a Specific Skill

Weak framing: "I don't have much experience with Python programming."

Strong framing: "While my primary programming experience is in Java, I recognize the growing importance of Python in data analysis. To address this, I've been taking an online Python course and working on personal projects to apply my learning. This process has reinforced my ability to quickly adapt to new technologies. It's also given me a fresh perspective on programming concepts, which has actually improved my Java coding. I'm excited to continue expanding my programming skills and applying them to diverse projects."

4. Impatience with Lengthy Processes

Weak framing: "I get frustrated with long, drawn-out processes."

Strong framing: "I have a strong drive for efficiency, which sometimes made me impatient with lengthy processes. I've learned to channel this energy into process improvement initiatives. In my current role, I led a team that streamlined our reporting procedure, reducing the time required by 30% while maintaining accuracy. This experience taught me the value of understanding a process thoroughly before attempting to change it. Now, I see my desire for efficiency as a strength that can contribute to continuous improvement in an organization."

Additional Tips for Discussing Weaknesses

1. Be Genuine

Avoid cliché weaknesses like "I work too hard" or "I'm a perfectionist" unless you can discuss them in a truly authentic and insightful way.

2. Show Continued Growth
Emphasize that you view improvement as an ongoing process. This demonstrates a growth mindset.

3. Avoid Crucial Job Skills
Don't mention weaknesses in areas that are fundamental to the job you're applying for.

4. Use the Present Perfect Tense
Phrases like "I have been working on…" or "I have learned to…" show ongoing improvement.

5. Prepare Multiple Weaknesses
Have 2-3 weaknesses prepared in case the interviewer asks for more than one.

6. Tailor to the Job
Consider the specific role and company when choosing which weaknesses to discuss.

7. Practice Your Delivery
Rehearse your responses to ensure you can discuss your weaknesses confidently and positively.

Conclusion

Discussing weaknesses in a job interview doesn't have to be a negative experience. By mastering the art of positive framing, you can turn this challenging question into an opportunity to showcase your self-awareness, adaptability, and commitment to personal growth. Remember, everyone has weaknesses; what sets exceptional candidates apart is their ability to

10. TURNING WEAKNESSES INTO STRENGTHS: THE ART OF POSITIVE...

recognize, address, and learn from these areas for improvement.

When you approach the weakness question with honesty, self-reflection, and a focus on growth, you demonstrate valuable qualities that employers seek: emotional intelligence, problem-solving skills, and a drive for continuous improvement. By effectively framing your weaknesses, you not only answer the question at hand but also provide a compelling narrative of personal and professional development that can significantly enhance your overall interview performance.

11. Quantifying Your Achievements for Maximum Impact

In the competitive landscape of job interviews, simply stating your accomplishments isn't enough. To truly stand out, you need to quantify your achievements, providing concrete evidence of your impact and value. This chapter will explore the art of quantifying your accomplishments to create powerful, memorable responses that resonate with interviewers.

The Power of Quantification

Quantifying your achievements:

1. Provides tangible evidence of your capabilities
2. Makes your accomplishments more memorable
3. Demonstrates your understanding of business metrics
4. Helps interviewers visualize your potential impact in their organization

Key Metrics for Quantification

1. Financial Metrics
   - Revenue increase
   - Cost savings
   - Profit margin improvement

11. QUANTIFYING YOUR ACHIEVEMENTS FOR MAXIMUM IMPACT

2. Efficiency Metrics
   - Time saved
   - Productivity increase
   - Error rate reduction

3. Growth Metrics
   - Market share increase
   - Customer acquisition
   - User base growth

4. Quality Metrics
   - Customer satisfaction scores
   - Product defect reduction
   - Service level improvements

5. Project Metrics
   - On-time completion rates
   - Budget adherence
   - Scope expansion

Strategies for Effective Quantification

1. Use Specific Numbers
   Instead of saying "I increased sales significantly," say "I increased sales by 35% over six months."

2. Provide Context
   Explain what the numbers mean in the broader context of your role or the company.

Example: "I increased customer retention by 20%, which translated to an additional $500,000 in annual recurring revenue."

3. Use Percentages and Absolute Numbers

Combine percentages and absolute numbers for maximum impact.

Example: "I reduced operational costs by 15%, saving the company $300,000 annually."

4. Highlight Before and After

Showcase the change you effected by presenting before and after figures.

Example: "I improved team productivity from 65% to 92% efficiency within three months."

5. Emphasize Your Direct Contribution

Make it clear how your actions led to the quantified result.

Example: "Through the implementation of a new CRM system that I championed and oversaw, we increased lead conversion rates by 40%."

6. Use Industry Benchmarks

If possible, compare your achievements to industry standards to provide additional context.

Example: "I achieved a customer satisfaction score of 95%, which is 20 points above the industry average."

7. Showcase Consistent Performance

If applicable, demonstrate sustained success over time.

Example: "I exceeded sales targets by an average of 25% each quarter for two consecutive years."

8. Highlight Indirect Impact

Sometimes your achievements indirectly affect other areas. Quantify these

11. QUANTIFYING YOUR ACHIEVEMENTS FOR MAXIMUM IMPACT

as well.

Example: "My marketing campaign increased website traffic by 150%, which led to a 30% boost in online sales."

Examples of Quantified Achievements Across Different Fields

1. Sales
   Weak: "I was a top performer in my sales team."
   Strong: "I consistently ranked in the top 5% of sales representatives, exceeding my annual quota by 135% and generating $2.5 million in new business over 18 months."

2. Marketing
   Weak: "I improved our social media presence."
   Strong: "I developed and implemented a comprehensive social media strategy that increased our follower base by 200% across platforms, resulting in a 45% increase in website traffic and a 25% boost in lead generation within six months."

3. Project Management
   Weak: "I successfully managed multiple projects."
   Strong: "I simultaneously led five cross-functional projects with a combined budget of $3 million, delivering all projects on time and 10% under budget, which saved the company $300,000."

4. Human Resources
   Weak: "I improved our hiring process."
   Strong: "I redesigned our recruitment strategy, reducing time-to-hire by 40% (from 50 to 30 days) and increasing new hire retention rates from 75% to 90% over a one-year period, saving an estimated $200,000 in recruitment and training costs."

5. Customer Service

Weak: "I resolved customer complaints effectively."

Strong: "I achieved a 98% customer satisfaction rate, handling an average of 50 complex inquiries daily. My resolution strategies were adopted company-wide, contributing to a 15% increase in overall customer retention."

6. Software Development

Weak: "I improved our app's performance."

Strong: "I optimized our mobile app's loading time by 60%, reducing it from 5 seconds to 2 seconds. This improvement led to a 25% increase in daily active users and a 40% decrease in app abandonment rates within three months of implementation."

7. Finance

Weak: "I identified cost-saving opportunities."

Strong: "I conducted a comprehensive audit of vendor contracts, identifying and implementing cost-saving measures that reduced annual expenses by $1.2 million, equivalent to 8% of the company's operational budget."

8. Operations

Weak: "I streamlined our manufacturing process."

Strong: "I led a lean manufacturing initiative that increased production efficiency by 30%, reduced waste by 25%, and lowered production costs by $500,000 annually, while maintaining our 99.9% quality assurance standards."

Techniques for Uncovering Quantifiable Achievements

1. Review Past Performance Evaluations

Look for metrics or achievements highlighted in your past reviews.

2. Analyze Project Outcomes

Examine the results of projects you've worked on, focusing on measurable impacts.

11. QUANTIFYING YOUR ACHIEVEMENTS FOR MAXIMUM IMPACT

3. Check Company Reports

If available, review company reports or presentations that might mention initiatives you were involved in.

4. Reconstruct Timelines

Create a timeline of your tenure in each role, noting key projects and their outcomes.

5. Consult with Colleagues

Reach out to former colleagues or supervisors to help you recall specific achievements and their impact.

6. Examine Industry Standards

Research industry benchmarks to understand how your performance compares.

7. Review Job Descriptions

Look at the metrics mentioned in job descriptions for your roles to identify relevant areas of quantification.

Tips for Presenting Quantified Achievements in Interviews

1. Prepare a Range

If you're not certain of exact figures, prepare a range. For example, "I increased efficiency by 20-25%."

2. Be Prepared to Explain

Be ready to discuss how you arrived at your figures and what methods you used to measure success.

3. Use Visual Aids

If appropriate, consider bringing a portfolio or presentation with graphs or charts illustrating your achievements.

4. Tailor to the Role

Focus on quantified achievements that are most relevant to the position you're applying for.

5. Practice Delivery

Rehearse discussing your quantified achievements so you can present them confidently and naturally.

6. Be Honest

Never exaggerate or fabricate numbers. Stick to achievements you can verify if asked.

7. Show Progression

If possible, demonstrate growth over time with your quantified achievements.

Conclusion

Quantifying your achievements is a powerful way to differentiate yourself in job interviews. By presenting concrete, measurable results, you provide clear evidence of your capabilities and potential value to prospective employers. Remember, the goal is not just to impress with numbers, but to tell a compelling story of your impact and effectiveness in previous roles.

As you prepare for interviews, take the time to thoroughly review your career history and identify key achievements that can be quantified. Use the strategies and examples provided in this chapter to frame your accomplishments in a way that resonates with interviewers and aligns with the requirements of the role you're seeking.

By mastering the art of quantification, you transform your interview responses from vague statements into powerful demonstrations of your professional impact. This approach not only makes your achievements

11. QUANTIFYING YOUR ACHIEVEMENTS FOR MAXIMUM IMPACT

more memorable but also positions you as a results-oriented candidate who understands the metrics that matter in business. With practice and preparation, you'll be able to confidently present your quantified achievements, setting yourself apart as a high-impact candidate in any interview situation.

12. Body Language and Non-Verbal Communication in Interviews

While what you say in an interview is crucial, how you say it can be equally important. Non-verbal communication, including body language, facial expressions, and tone of voice, plays a significant role in how you're perceived by interviewers. Mastering these non-verbal cues can dramatically enhance your interview performance and help you build rapport with potential employers.

The Importance of Non-Verbal Communication

Non-verbal cues account for a substantial portion of our communication. They can:

1. Reinforce or contradict your verbal messages
2. Convey confidence and competence
3. Demonstrate your level of interest and engagement
4. Build trust and rapport with the interviewer

Key Elements of Non-Verbal Communication in Interviews

1. Eye Contact

12. BODY LANGUAGE AND NON-VERBAL COMMUNICATION IN INTERVIEWS

Maintaining appropriate eye contact is crucial for establishing trust and showing confidence.

Do:
  - Make consistent eye contact throughout the interview
  - In panel interviews, make eye contact with all interviewers, focusing on the person asking the question
  - Look away occasionally to avoid staring

Don't:
  - Avoid eye contact, which can signal dishonesty or lack of confidence
  - Overdo it, as constant eye contact can be perceived as aggressive

2. Facial Expressions

Your facial expressions should convey interest, enthusiasm, and positivity.

Do:
  - Smile genuinely when appropriate
  - Show attentiveness through your expressions
  - Mirror the interviewer's expressions to build rapport

Don't:
  - Frown or scowl, which can indicate displeasure or confusion
  - Maintain a blank expression, which can be interpreted as disinterest

3. Posture

Your posture can communicate confidence and professionalism.

Do:
  - Sit up straight with your shoulders back
  - Lean slightly forward to show engagement

- Keep your feet firmly on the ground

Don't:
  - Slouch, which can indicate laziness or disinterest
  - Cross your arms, which can appear defensive
  - Fidget or shift constantly, which can signal nervousness

4. Hand Gestures

Using hand gestures can emphasize points and make your communication more dynamic.

Do:
  - Use open hand gestures to appear honest and open
  - Keep gestures within the frame of your body
  - Use gestures to emphasize key points

Don't:
  - Use excessive or wild gestures, which can be distracting
  - Point directly at the interviewer, which can seem aggressive
  - Play with objects (pens, jewelry) as this indicates nervousness

5. Tone of Voice

Your vocal tone can convey confidence, enthusiasm, and sincerity.

Do:
  - Speak clearly and at a moderate pace
  - Vary your tone to maintain interest
  - Use a confident, assertive tone

Don't:
  - Speak too softly, which can indicate lack of confidence

12. BODY LANGUAGE AND NON-VERBAL COMMUNICATION IN INTERVIEWS

- Use a monotone voice, which can seem disinterested
- Speak too quickly, which can indicate nervousness

6. Handshake

A handshake is often the first and last physical contact you'll have with an interviewer.

Do:
- Offer a firm, brief handshake
- Make eye contact and smile while shaking hands
- Wait for the interviewer to extend their hand first

Don't:
- Give a limp or overly strong handshake
- Avoid eye contact during the handshake
- Offer a sweaty palm (discreetly wipe your hand first if needed)

7. Personal Space

Respecting personal space is crucial for making others comfortable.

Do:
- Maintain an appropriate distance (about arm's length) from the interviewer
- Adjust your position if the interviewer seems uncomfortable

Don't:
- Invade the interviewer's personal space
- Sit too far away, which can create a sense of disconnection

Strategies for Improving Non-Verbal Communication

1. Practice in Front of a Mirror
Observe your facial expressions, posture, and gestures as you answer common interview questions.

2. Record Yourself
Video record a mock interview to analyze your non-verbal cues objectively.

3. Seek Feedback
Ask a friend or mentor to observe your body language during a mock interview and provide constructive feedback.

4. Be Mindful of Cultural Differences
Research and be aware of any cultural differences in non-verbal communication, especially for international interviews.

5. Dress Appropriately
Wear professional attire that makes you feel confident and comfortable.

6. Arrive Early
Arrive at least 10-15 minutes early to compose yourself and adjust to the environment.

7. Take Deep Breaths
Use deep breathing techniques before and during the interview to calm nerves and maintain composure.

8. Stay Present
Focus on the present moment and actively listen to the interviewer, which naturally improves your non-verbal cues.

9. Prepare Thoroughly
The more prepared you are with your responses, the more confident your body language will be.

12. BODY LANGUAGE AND NON-VERBAL COMMUNICATION IN INTERVIEWS

Common Non-Verbal Mistakes to Avoid

1. Checking Your Phone
This shows disinterest and disrespect. Keep your phone off and out of sight.

2. Poor Grooming
Unkempt appearance can indicate a lack of professionalism. Ensure you're well-groomed and presentable.

3. Lack of Smile
While you shouldn't smile constantly, a lack of smiling can make you appear unfriendly or disinterested.

4. Weak Handshake
A limp handshake can indicate a lack of confidence or enthusiasm.

5. Nervous Habits
Avoid habits like nail-biting, hair twirling, or leg shaking, which display nervousness.

6. Poor Posture
Slouching or hunching over can indicate a lack of confidence or interest.

7. Lack of Eye Contact
Avoiding eye contact can be interpreted as dishonesty or insecurity.

8. Crossing Arms
This can appear defensive or closed off.

9. Invading Personal Space
Standing or sitting too close can make the interviewer uncomfortable.

10. Excessive Nodding

While nodding shows agreement, excessive nodding can appear insincere or overeager.

Adapting to Different Interview Formats

1. Video Interviews
   - Ensure good lighting and a professional background
   - Look directly into the camera to simulate eye contact
   - Sit far enough back so your upper body is visible for gestures
   - Be aware of your facial expressions, as they're more prominent on video

2. Phone Interviews
   - Stand up or sit straight to project confidence in your voice
   - Smile while speaking to inject warmth into your tone
   - Use verbal affirmations to show you're engaged, as the interviewer can't see your non-verbal cues

3. Panel Interviews
   - Make eye contact with all panel members, not just the person asking the question
   - Be aware of your body language when not speaking, as you're always visible to someone

4. Informal Interviews (e.g., coffee meetings)
   - Maintain professionalism despite the casual setting
   - Be mindful of your posture and gestures, even in a more relaxed environment

Conclusion

Mastering non-verbal communication can significantly enhance your interview performance. Your body language and other non-verbal cues should

12. BODY LANGUAGE AND NON-VERBAL COMMUNICATION IN INTERVIEWS

align with and reinforce your verbal responses, presenting a coherent, confident, and engaged persona to the interviewer.

Remember that non-verbal communication is a two-way street. While focusing on your own body language, also pay attention to the interviewer's non-verbal cues. This can provide valuable insights into how your responses are being received and allow you to adjust your approach if necessary.

Practice is key to improving your non-verbal communication skills. The more you rehearse and become aware of your non-verbal habits, the more natural and confident you'll appear in the actual interview. By presenting a consistent message through both your words and your body language, you'll create a powerful, positive impression that can set you apart from other candidates and significantly increase your chances of interview success.

13. Mastering the Art of Storytelling in Your Responses

Storytelling is a powerful tool in job interviews. It can transform your responses from dry recitations of facts into compelling narratives that engage the interviewer and make your experiences memorable. Mastering the art of storytelling in your interview responses can significantly enhance your chances of standing out and leaving a lasting impression.

Why Storytelling Matters in Interviews

1. Memorable: Stories are more memorable than plain facts or statements.
2. Engaging: Narratives capture and maintain the interviewer's attention.
3. Demonstrative: Stories show rather than tell, providing concrete examples of your skills and experiences.
4. Emotional Connection: Well-told stories can create an emotional connection with the interviewer.
5. Differentiation: Storytelling sets you apart from candidates who provide generic responses.

Elements of Effective Interview Stories

13. MASTERING THE ART OF STORYTELLING IN YOUR RESPONSES

1. Relevance: The story should directly relate to the question or job requirement.
2. Structure: A clear beginning, middle, and end.
3. Brevity: Concise enough to maintain interest but detailed enough to be impactful.
4. Conflict or Challenge: A problem or obstacle that needed to be overcome.
5. Action: Your specific role and actions in addressing the challenge.
6. Result: The positive outcome or lessons learned from the experience.
7. Reflection: What you gained or how you grew from the experience.

The STAR Method in Storytelling

The STAR method (Situation, Task, Action, Result) is an excellent framework for structuring your interview stories:

Situation: Set the scene and provide context.
   Task: Explain the challenge or objective you faced.
   Action: Describe the specific steps you took to address the situation.
   Result: Share the outcomes of your actions and any lessons learned.

Crafting Compelling Interview Stories

1. Identify Key Experiences
Review your resume and career history to identify experiences that showcase your skills and align with common interview questions.

2. Prepare a Story Bank
Develop a repertoire of 5-7 adaptable stories that can be tailored to various interview questions.

3. Focus on Challenges and Growth

Highlight situations where you faced difficulties and how you overcame them, demonstrating resilience and problem-solving skills.

4. Use Specific Details
Include concrete details to make your story vivid and believable, but avoid unnecessary information that doesn't add value.

5. Practice Your Delivery
Rehearse your stories out loud to refine your delivery and ensure you can tell them naturally and concisely.

6. Tailor to the Job
Adapt your stories to emphasize aspects most relevant to the position you're applying for.

Example of a Well-Crafted Interview Story

Question: "Tell me about a time when you had to deal with a difficult team member."

Poor Response: "I once had a coworker who was always late with their work. I talked to them about it, and things got better."

Effective Storytelling Response:

"In my previous role as a project manager at XYZ Corp, we were working on a critical software update with a tight six-week deadline (Situation). As the project lead, I was responsible for ensuring all team members met their milestones to keep us on track (Task).

About two weeks into the project, I noticed that one of our senior developers consistently missed internal deadlines and was often defensive when asked about his progress. This was putting our entire timeline at risk (Conflict).

13. MASTERING THE ART OF STORYTELLING IN YOUR RESPONSES

I decided to approach the situation carefully. First, I scheduled a one-on-one meeting with the developer in a neutral setting – a coffee shop near our office. I started by asking if there were any challenges he was facing that I might not be aware of (Action).

Through this conversation, I discovered that he was struggling with a particularly complex coding issue and felt embarrassed to ask for help, given his senior status. I assured him that seeking assistance was not a sign of weakness but a normal part of the development process.

Together, we developed a plan. I paired him with another experienced developer who could provide guidance without making him feel subordinate. I also implemented daily quick check-ins to catch any issues early and adjusted our project management software to break his tasks into smaller, more manageable chunks (Action).

As a result of these changes, the developer's productivity improved significantly. He completed his portion of the project on time, and we successfully launched the software update two days ahead of schedule (Result).

This experience reinforced for me the importance of open communication and creating an environment where team members feel comfortable asking for help. It also improved my ability to recognize and address potential issues before they escalate. In subsequent projects, I implemented regular one-on-one check-ins with all team members, which has led to smoother project execution and stronger team cohesion (Reflection)."

Tips for Effective Storytelling in Interviews

1. Start Strong
    Begin your story with an engaging opening that immediately captures the interviewer's attention.

2. Use Active Language
Employ action verbs and vivid descriptions to make your story more dynamic and engaging.

3. Show, Don't Tell
Instead of stating that you're a "good problem solver," tell a story that demonstrates this skill in action.

4. Include Dialogue
Where appropriate, include brief snippets of dialogue to make your story more vivid and personal.

5. Emphasize Your Role
While acknowledging team efforts, make sure to highlight your specific contributions and decision-making process.

6. Quantify Results
Whenever possible, include specific metrics or data to illustrate the impact of your actions.

7. End with Reflection
Conclude your story by sharing what you learned or how the experience shaped your professional growth.

8. Be Authentic
While it's important to present yourself in the best light, ensure your stories are truthful and genuine.

9. Adapt to Your Audience
Tailor your language and level of technical detail to your interviewer's background and the role you're applying for.

10. Practice Nonverbal Storytelling

13. MASTERING THE ART OF STORYTELLING IN YOUR RESPONSES

Use appropriate facial expressions, gestures, and tone of voice to enhance your narrative.

Avoiding Common Storytelling Pitfalls

1. Rambling
Stay focused on the key points of your story. If you find yourself going off on tangents, practice trimming your story to its essential elements.

2. Negativity
Even when discussing challenges, maintain a positive tone. Focus on solutions and growth rather than dwelling on problems.

3. Lack of Relevance
Ensure your story directly addresses the question asked and relates to the job you're applying for.

4. Overemphasis on Context
While setting the scene is important, don't spend too much time on background details. Get to the main action quickly.

5. Failure to Highlight Your Role
Make sure it's clear what your specific contributions were, especially in stories about team efforts.

6. Lack of Conclusion
Always wrap up your story with a clear result or lesson learned. Don't leave the interviewer wondering about the outcome.

Conclusion

Mastering the art of storytelling in your interview responses can transform your interview performance. By crafting compelling narratives that showcase your skills, experiences, and problem-solving abilities, you create a memorable impression that sets you apart from other candidates.

Remember, effective storytelling in interviews is about more than just recounting events. It's about strategically selecting and presenting experiences that demonstrate your qualifications for the role. With practice and preparation, you can develop a repertoire of powerful stories that not only answer interview questions but also paint a vivid picture of your professional capabilities and potential.

By incorporating storytelling techniques into your interview responses, you engage the interviewer on both an intellectual and emotional level, making your candidacy more compelling and memorable. This approach can significantly enhance your chances of success in any interview situation.

14. Acing Different Interview Formats: One-on-One, Panel, and Video

In today's job market, candidates must be prepared to excel in various interview formats. Each type of interview – one-on-one, panel, and video – presents unique challenges and opportunities. This chapter will explore strategies for succeeding in these different formats, helping you adapt your approach to showcase your best self regardless of the interview setting.

One-on-One Interviews

One-on-one interviews are the most common format, typically involving just you and a single interviewer.

Advantages:
 - More personal interaction
 - Easier to build rapport
 - Often more conversational in nature

Strategies for Success:

1. Build Rapport
   Take cues from the interviewer's demeanor to strike the right tone. If they're formal, maintain professionalism. If they're more casual, you can be

a bit more relaxed.

2. Use the Interviewer's Name
If appropriate, use the interviewer's name occasionally to personalize the conversation.

3. Pay Attention to Body Language
In a one-on-one setting, your body language is more noticeable. Maintain good posture, make appropriate eye contact, and use engaged facial expressions.

4. Ask Thoughtful Questions
Prepare specific questions about the role and company to demonstrate your interest and research.

5. Be Prepared for Silences
Don't feel pressured to fill every silence. Sometimes interviewers pause to take notes or consider their next question.

6. Follow the Interviewer's Lead
Be prepared to go into depth on topics the interviewer seems particularly interested in.

7. Close Strongly
At the end of the interview, reiterate your interest in the position and ask about next steps.

Panel Interviews

Panel interviews involve multiple interviewers, often from different departments or levels within the organization.

Advantages:

- Efficient for the company
- Allows for diverse perspectives on your candidacy
- Can provide a broader view of the organization

Strategies for Success:

1. Research the Panel

If possible, find out who will be on the panel and their roles within the company. This can help you tailor your responses.

2. Address All Panel Members

Make eye contact with each panelist, not just the person asking the question. When answering, begin by looking at the questioner, but then make eye contact with others as well.

3. Remember Names

Try to remember and use panelists' names when appropriate. This personalizes your responses and shows attentiveness.

4. Be Prepared for Varied Questions

Different panelists may focus on different aspects of your background or the role. Be ready to shift gears quickly.

5. Manage Group Dynamics

Be aware of the dynamics between panel members. If there's a clear leader, make sure to address them respectfully without ignoring others.

6. Handle Rapid-Fire Questions

Sometimes panel interviews can feel like a barrage of questions. Stay calm and take a moment to collect your thoughts if needed.

7. Bring Extra Copies of Your Resume

Have enough copies for all panel members, plus a few extra.

8. Follow Up Individually

If possible, send personalized thank-you notes to each panel member, referencing specific points from your conversation with them.

Video Interviews

Video interviews, conducted via platforms like Zoom or Skype, have become increasingly common, especially for initial rounds or remote positions.

Advantages:
  - Convenient for both parties
  - Allows for interviews across geographic boundaries
  - Can be recorded for review by other team members

Strategies for Success:

1. Test Your Technology

Well before the interview, test your internet connection, camera, and microphone. Have a backup plan (like a phone number to call) in case of technical issues.

2. Choose an Appropriate Setting

Select a quiet location with a neutral background. Ensure good lighting, ideally with natural light facing you.

3. Dress Professionally

Dress as you would for an in-person interview, including bottoms (in case you need to stand up).

4. Make "Eye Contact" with the Camera

Look directly into the camera when speaking to simulate eye contact. It's tempting to watch yourself or the interviewer on screen, but this can make you appear distracted.

14. ACING DIFFERENT INTERVIEW FORMATS: ONE-ON-ONE, PANEL,...

5. Minimize Distractions

Turn off notifications on your computer and phone. Ensure pets, family members, or roommates won't interrupt.

6. Use Notes Carefully

It's okay to have notes, but don't rely on them too heavily. Glancing down frequently can make you appear unprepared.

7. Practice Your Video Presence

Conduct mock interviews via video to get comfortable with the format and to check how you appear on camera.

8. Be Aware of Body Language

Non-verbal cues can be more challenging to read on video. Use clear facial expressions and occasional hand gestures to convey engagement.

9. Speak Clearly and at a Moderate Pace

Audio can sometimes lag or cut out. Speak clearly and at a slightly slower pace than you might in person.

10. Have a Glass of Water Handy

Keep water nearby in case your throat gets dry, but be cautious when drinking on camera.

General Tips for All Interview Formats

1. Prepare Thoroughly

Regardless of the format, thorough preparation is key. Research the company, practice common questions, and prepare your own questions.

2. Arrive or Log In Early

For in-person interviews, arrive 10-15 minutes early. For video interviews, log in 5-10 minutes before the scheduled time.

3. Bring Materials

Have copies of your resume, a notepad, and a pen. For video interviews, have these items neatly arranged off-camera.

4. Listen Actively

Pay close attention to questions and comments. Don't hesitate to ask for clarification if needed.

5. Use the STAR Method

For behavioral questions, use the Situation, Task, Action, Result format to structure your responses.

6. Be Authentic

While it's important to present your best self, be genuine in your responses and demeanor.

7. Show Enthusiasm

Demonstrate your interest in the role and company, regardless of the interview format.

8. Follow Up

Send a thank-you email within 24 hours of the interview, regardless of the format.

Adapting to Unexpected Formats

Sometimes you may encounter unexpected interview formats or last-minute changes. Here are some tips for adapting:

1. Stay Flexible

If the format changes (e.g., from one-on-one to panel), remain calm and adaptable.

14. ACING DIFFERENT INTERVIEW FORMATS: ONE-ON-ONE, PANEL,...

2. Ask for Clarification

If you're unsure about the format or what to expect, it's okay to ask for more information.

3. Bring Extra Materials

Always be prepared with extra copies of your resume and other relevant documents.

4. Be Ready for Anything

Mental preparation for various scenarios can help you stay confident if unexpected changes occur.

Conclusion

Each interview format presents its own set of challenges and opportunities. By understanding the nuances of one-on-one, panel, and video interviews, and preparing accordingly, you can adapt your approach to shine in any setting. Remember, regardless of the format, the core principles of effective interviewing remain the same: thorough preparation, clear communication, professional demeanor, and genuine enthusiasm for the opportunity.

Mastering these different formats will not only help you perform better in interviews but also demonstrate your adaptability and communication skills – qualities highly valued by employers. As you prepare for your next interview, consider the format and tailor your preparation accordingly. With practice and the right strategies, you can ace any interview format and move confidently towards your career goals.

15. The Post-Interview Playbook: Following Up and Negotiating Offers

The interview process doesn't end when you walk out of the room or log off the video call. What you do after the interview can be just as crucial as the interview itself. This chapter will guide you through the essential steps of following up after an interview and navigating the offer negotiation process.

Part 1: Following Up After the Interview

1. Send a Thank-You Note

Timing: Within 24 hours of the interview
   Purpose: To express appreciation, reiterate interest, and stay fresh in the interviewer's mind

Key elements of an effective thank-you note:
   - Express genuine gratitude for the interviewer's time
   - Reiterate your enthusiasm for the position
   - Briefly remind them of your key qualifications
   - Reference specific points from the conversation
   - Keep it concise (no more than a paragraph or two)

Example:

15. THE POST-INTERVIEW PLAYBOOK: FOLLOWING UP AND...

"Dear Ms. Johnson,

Thank you for taking the time to meet with me yesterday regarding the Marketing Manager position at XYZ Corp. I thoroughly enjoyed our conversation about the company's plans to expand into the Asian market, and I'm even more excited about the possibility of contributing to this initiative. As we discussed, my experience in developing successful marketing strategies for international markets aligns well with your goals. I'm particularly enthusiastic about applying my knowledge of social media trends in Southeast Asia to help drive your expansion efforts.

Thank you again for your time and consideration. I look forward to hearing about the next steps in the process.

Best regards,
 [Your Name]"

2. Connect on LinkedIn

If appropriate, send a connection request to your interviewer on LinkedIn. This helps maintain a professional connection and keeps you on their radar.

3. Provide Any Requested Follow-Up Materials

If the interviewer asked for additional information or samples of your work, send these promptly.

4. Be Patient, But Proactive

If you haven't heard back within the timeframe they specified, it's appropriate to send a polite follow-up email inquiring about the status of your application.

Part 2: Negotiating Offers

Receiving a job offer is exciting, but it's important to approach the negotiation process strategically.

1. Express Enthusiasm and Gratitude

Always start by expressing your appreciation for the offer and your excitement about the opportunity.

2. Ask for Time to Consider the Offer

It's perfectly acceptable to ask for a few days to review the offer. This gives you time to evaluate it thoroughly and prepare for negotiations.

3. Evaluate the Entire Package

Consider all aspects of the offer:
  - Base salary
  - Bonuses and incentives
  - Health benefits
  - Retirement plans
  - Vacation time and paid time off
  - Professional development opportunities
  - Work-life balance (e.g., flexible hours, remote work options)
  - Career growth potential

4. Research Market Rates

Use resources like Glassdoor, PayScale, and industry reports to understand the typical salary range for the position in your area.

5. Prioritize Your Needs

Determine what's most important to you. Is it base salary, flexible working hours, or professional development opportunities?

6. Prepare Your Case

Develop a clear rationale for your requests based on:
 - Your qualifications and experience
 - The value you'll bring to the company
 - Market rates for similar positions
 - Any unique skills or perspectives you offer

7. Practice Your Negotiation

Rehearse your negotiation pitch with a friend or mentor. Be prepared to articulate your value proposition clearly and confidently.

8. Initiate the Negotiation Conversation

Contact the hiring manager or HR representative to discuss the offer. It's often best to have this conversation over the phone or in person rather than via email.

9. Start with Your Highest Priority

Begin the negotiation with your most important request. Be prepared to explain why it's important to you and how it aligns with the company's interests.

Example:
 "Thank you for the offer. I'm very excited about the opportunity to join your team. Based on my research and the value I believe I can bring to the role, I was hoping we could discuss the possibility of adjusting the base salary to [specific amount]. Given my experience in [relevant area] and my track record of [specific achievement], I believe this would be in line with the

market rate for this position."

10. Be Prepared to Compromise

Negotiation is a give-and-take process. Be open to alternative forms of compensation if your primary request can't be met.

11. Get the Final Offer in Writing

Once you've reached an agreement, ask for an updated offer letter that includes all the agreed-upon terms.

12. Respond Promptly

Once you're satisfied with the offer, respond promptly with your acceptance.

Common Negotiation Mistakes to Avoid:

1. Accepting the first offer without negotiation
2. Focusing solely on salary and ignoring other benefits
3. Making ultimatums or using aggressive tactics
4. Providing personal reasons (e.g., debt, cost of living) as justification for higher pay
5. Neglecting to get the final agreement in writing

Handling Rejection

If the company decides not to move forward with your candidacy:

1. Respond graciously, thanking them for their time and consideration.

15. THE POST-INTERVIEW PLAYBOOK: FOLLOWING UP AND...

2. Ask for feedback on your interview performance, if appropriate.
3. Express interest in being considered for future opportunities if you're still interested in the company.
4. Maintain the professional connection by staying in touch via LinkedIn or industry events.

Conclusion

The post-interview phase is a critical part of the job search process. A well-crafted follow-up can reinforce a positive impression and keep you top-of-mind for the position. If you receive an offer, approaching the negotiation process with preparation, professionalism, and clarity can help you secure a package that aligns with your worth and career goals.

Remember, the goal of negotiation is to reach a mutually beneficial agreement. By articulating your value, understanding the company's perspective, and maintaining a positive, professional demeanor throughout the process, you set the stage for a successful start to your new role.

Whether you're writing a thank-you note, following up on an application status, or negotiating an offer, always maintain professionalism, express gratitude, and focus on the value you bring to the organization. These post-interview strategies can significantly impact your job search success and help you start your new position on the right foot.

16. Industry-Specific Interview Guides: Tech, Finance, Healthcare, and More

Many interview principles are universal, each industry has its own nuances and expectations. This chapter provides tailored guidance for interviews in technology, finance, healthcare, and other key sectors, helping you prepare for industry-specific challenges and questions.

Technology Industry

Key Focus Areas:

1. Technical skills and knowledge
2. Problem-solving abilities
3. Adaptability to rapid technological changes
4. Collaboration in cross-functional teams

Common Interview Elements:

1. Technical interviews
2. Coding challenges
3. System design questions
4. Behavioral interviews

16. INDUSTRY-SPECIFIC INTERVIEW GUIDES: TECH, FINANCE,...

Preparation Tips:

1. Stay updated on the latest technologies and industry trends
2. Practice coding problems on platforms like LeetCode or HackerRank
3. Be prepared to explain your problem-solving process
4. Familiarize yourself with the company's tech stack and products

Sample Questions:

1. "Explain the concept of object-oriented programming and its benefits."
2. "How would you design a scalable system for a social media platform?"
3. "Describe a time when you had to learn a new technology quickly for a project."

Tips for Success:

1. Showcase your passion for technology and continuous learning
2. Highlight any open-source contributions or personal projects
3. Demonstrate your ability to explain complex concepts simply
4. Be prepared to whiteboard or share your screen for coding exercises

Finance Industry

Key Focus Areas:

1. Analytical and quantitative skills
2. Understanding of financial markets and instruments
3. Regulatory knowledge
4. Attention to detail and ethical conduct

Common Interview Elements:

1. Technical finance questions
2. Market knowledge assessments
3. Behavioral interviews
4. Case studies or financial modeling exercises

Preparation Tips:

1. Stay informed about current financial news and market trends
2. Review key financial concepts and formulas
3. Practice financial modeling and valuation techniques
4. Understand the specific sector of finance you're interviewing for (e.g., investment banking, corporate finance, risk management)

Sample Questions:

1. "Walk me through a discounted cash flow (DCF) analysis."
2. "How would you evaluate the financial health of a company?"
3. "Explain how changes in interest rates affect different financial instruments."

Tips for Success:

1. Demonstrate strong numerical and analytical skills
2. Show awareness of ethical considerations in finance
3. Highlight any relevant certifications (e.g., CFA, CPA)
4. Be prepared to discuss your views on market trends and economic factors

16. INDUSTRY-SPECIFIC INTERVIEW GUIDES: TECH, FINANCE,...

Healthcare Industry

Key Focus Areas:

1. Patient care and empathy
2. Knowledge of healthcare systems and regulations
3. Ability to work in multidisciplinary teams
4. Commitment to continuous learning and best practices

Common Interview Elements:

1. Clinical knowledge assessments (for clinical roles)
2. Scenario-based questions
3. Behavioral interviews
4. Compliance and ethics discussions

Preparation Tips:

1. Stay updated on healthcare policies and regulations
2. Familiarize yourself with the organization's mission and values
3. Prepare examples demonstrating patient-centric care or process improvements
4. Understand the challenges facing the healthcare industry

Sample Questions:

1. "How do you ensure patient confidentiality in your work?"
2. "Describe a time when you had to deal with a difficult patient or family member."
3. "How do you stay updated on the latest developments in healthcare?"

Tips for Success:

1. Emphasize your commitment to patient care and safety
2. Demonstrate your ability to work in diverse, multidisciplinary teams
3. Highlight any specialized skills or certifications relevant to the role
4. Show awareness of the importance of both empathy and efficiency in healthcare

Marketing and Advertising Industry

Key Focus Areas:

1. Creativity and innovation
2. Data-driven decision making
3. Understanding of digital platforms and emerging trends
4. Strategic thinking and campaign planning

Common Interview Elements:

1. Portfolio reviews
2. Case studies or campaign pitch exercises
3. Behavioral interviews
4. Assessments of market and consumer knowledge

Preparation Tips:

1. Prepare a compelling portfolio of your work
2. Stay updated on the latest marketing trends and technologies
3. Familiarize yourself with the company's brand and recent campaigns
4. Practice explaining your creative process and strategic thinking

Sample Questions:

1. "How would you measure the success of a marketing campaign?"
2. "Describe a time when you had to pivot a marketing strategy due to unexpected challenges."
3. "How do you stay creative and generate new ideas?"

Tips for Success:

1. Showcase your creativity and innovative thinking
2. Demonstrate your ability to blend creativity with data-driven insights
3. Highlight your adaptability to new platforms and technologies
4. Be prepared to discuss both successful and unsuccessful campaigns you've worked on

Education Sector

Key Focus Areas:

1. Passion for education and student development
2. Pedagogical knowledge and skills
3. Adaptability to diverse learning needs
4. Classroom management and communication skills

Common Interview Elements:

1. Teaching demonstrations or sample lessons
2. Scenario-based questions
3. Discussions on educational philosophy
4. Behavioral interviews

Preparation Tips:

1. Stay informed about current educational trends and policies
2. Prepare a teaching philosophy statement
3. Familiarize yourself with the institution's curriculum and values
4. Gather concrete examples of your teaching methods and their impacts

Sample Questions:

1. "How do you adapt your teaching style to accommodate different learning styles?"
2. "Describe how you would handle a student who is consistently disruptive in class."
3. "What strategies do you use to engage students and make learning fun?"

Tips for Success:

1. Demonstrate your passion for education and student success
2. Highlight your ability to create inclusive and engaging learning environments
3. Showcase your use of technology or innovative teaching methods
4. Emphasize your commitment to ongoing professional development

General Tips for Industry-Specific Interviews

1. Research the Company and Role Thoroughly
   Understand the company's position in the industry, its competitors, and recent developments. Tailor your responses to align with the company's goals and culture.

16. INDUSTRY-SPECIFIC INTERVIEW GUIDES: TECH, FINANCE,...

2. Prepare Industry-Specific Examples
Have concrete examples ready that demonstrate your expertise and achievements in the specific industry.

3. Show Awareness of Industry Trends and Challenges
Demonstrate your knowledge of current industry trends, challenges, and potential future developments.

4. Highlight Relevant Skills and Experiences
Focus on the skills and experiences most valued in the industry, even if they're from different sectors or roles.

5. Ask Thoughtful Industry-Specific Questions
Prepare questions that show your insight into the industry and genuine interest in the role and company.

6. Demonstrate Adaptability
Highlight your ability to adapt to industry changes, whether technological, regulatory, or market-driven.

7. Emphasize Continuous Learning
Show your commitment to staying updated in your field through certifications, courses, or self-study.

8. Understand the Industry's Regulatory Environment
Demonstrate awareness of key regulations or compliance issues relevant to the industry.

9. Speak the Industry Language
Use industry-specific terminology appropriately to showcase your familiarity with the field.

10. Connect Your Past Experiences to the New Role

Even if you're changing industries, find ways to relate your past experiences to the challenges and needs of the new industry.

Conclusion

While the core principles of interviewing remain consistent across industries, understanding and preparing for industry-specific nuances can give you a significant advantage. By tailoring your preparation to the specific sector you're interviewing in, you demonstrate not just your skills and experience, but also your genuine interest and fit for the industry.

Remember, industries are constantly evolving, so staying current with trends, challenges, and innovations in your chosen field is crucial. Combine this industry-specific knowledge with strong general interviewing skills, and you'll be well-equipped to excel in any interview, regardless of the sector.

17. 25 Smart Questions to Ask Your Interviewer

Asking thoughtful questions during an interview is not just an opportunity to gather information; it's a chance to demonstrate your interest, insight, and preparation. Here are 25 smart questions to consider asking your interviewer, along with explanations of why they're effective and how to use them strategically.

1. "What does a typical day look like in this role?"
This question shows your interest in the day-to-day responsibilities and helps you understand what to expect if you get the job.

2. "What are the biggest challenges facing the team/department right now?"
This demonstrates your forward-thinking approach and desire to understand current priorities.

3. "How does this position contribute to the overall company goals?"
This question shows that you're thinking about the bigger picture and how you can add value to the organization.

4. "Can you tell me about the team I'll be working with?"
This helps you understand the team dynamics and shows your interest in collaboration.

5. "What opportunities for professional development does the company offer?"

This demonstrates your commitment to growth and long-term career planning.

6. "How would you describe the company culture?"

This shows your interest in finding a good cultural fit and understanding the work environment.

7. "What does success look like in this role, and how is it measured?"

This question demonstrates your results-oriented mindset and desire to excel in the position.

8. "How has this role evolved since it was created?"

This shows your interest in the position's history and potential future direction.

9. "What are the company's plans for growth and development in the next few years?"

This demonstrates your long-term interest in the company and industry awareness.

10. "Can you tell me about a project or initiative you're particularly proud of?"

This allows the interviewer to share positive experiences and gives you insight into what the company values.

11. "How does the company support work-life balance?"

This shows your interest in maintaining a healthy balance while being productive.

12. "What are the next steps in the interview process?"

This demonstrates your enthusiasm for moving forward and helps you understand the timeline.

13. "How does the company approach innovation and staying competitive in the industry?"
This shows your forward-thinking mindset and interest in the company's strategic approach.

14. "Can you tell me about the onboarding process for new employees?"
This demonstrates your eagerness to integrate quickly and effectively into the role.

15. "What opportunities are there for cross-departmental collaboration?"
This shows your interest in working across teams and understanding the broader organization.

16. "How does the company handle feedback and employee suggestions?"
This demonstrates your interest in contributing ideas and your value for open communication.

17. "What are the most important qualities for someone to excel in this role?"
This helps you understand the key attributes the company is looking for and allows you to highlight how you match these.

18. "How has the company adapted to recent industry changes or challenges?"
This shows your awareness of industry trends and interest in the company's adaptability.

19. "Can you tell me about the company's approach to diversity and inclusion?"
This demonstrates your value for a diverse workplace and interest in the company's cultural initiatives.

20. "What are the opportunities for advancement within the company?"

This shows your interest in long-term career growth within the organization.

21. "How does the company support employees' charitable or community involvement?"
This demonstrates your interest in corporate social responsibility and community engagement.

22. "What's your favorite part about working here?"
This personal question can provide insight into the company culture and employee satisfaction.

23. "How does the company stay connected and maintain team cohesion, especially with remote work?"
This shows awareness of modern work challenges and interest in team dynamics.

24. "Can you tell me about a time when an employee demonstrated one of the company's core values?"
This demonstrates your interest in understanding how the company's values are put into practice.

25. "What has been the most surprising or unexpected aspect of working here for you?"
This can provide unique insights into the company and shows your curiosity about the employee experience.

Strategies for Asking Questions Effectively:

1. Tailor Questions to the Interview Stage
In initial interviews, focus on broader questions about the role and company. Save more specific or in-depth questions for later stages.

17. 25 SMART QUESTIONS TO ASK YOUR INTERVIEWER

2. Listen Actively and Ask Follow-up Questions
Show that you're engaged by asking follow-up questions based on the interviewer's responses.

3. Prioritize Your Questions
Have your most important questions ready in case time is limited.

4. Avoid Questions with Obvious Answers
Don't ask questions that can be easily answered by looking at the company website or job description.

5. Be Mindful of Timing
Spread your questions throughout the interview if possible, rather than saving them all for the end.

6. Adapt to the Interviewer's Style
If the interviewer seems pressed for time, stick to concise, high-priority questions.

7. Show Genuine Interest
Your tone and body language should convey sincere curiosity and enthusiasm.

8. Avoid Premature Questions About Benefits or Salary
Unless the interviewer brings it up, save questions about compensation and benefits for later stages of the process.

9. Take Notes
Jot down key points from the interviewer's answers to show you're engaged and to help you remember important information.

10. Thank the Interviewer for Their Insights
Express appreciation for the information shared, reinforcing a positive

interaction.

Using Questions Strategically:

1. Demonstrate Research
Ask questions that show you've done your homework about the company and industry.

Example: "I read about your recent expansion into the Asian market. How does this role contribute to that growth strategy?"

2. Highlight Your Skills
Frame questions in a way that allows you to subtly emphasize your relevant skills or experiences.

Example: "In my previous role, I led a team that implemented a new CRM system. How does this company approach technology upgrades and process improvements?"

3. Address Potential Concerns
If you're concerned about a potential gap in your qualifications, ask a question that allows you to address it indirectly.

Example: "While my background is primarily in B2B marketing, I'm excited about transitioning to B2C. How does the company support employees in developing new skills or transitioning to different areas?"

4. Gauge Cultural Fit
Ask questions that help you understand if the company culture aligns with your values and work style.

Example: "Can you tell me about a recent team-building or company culture initiative that you found particularly effective?"

17. 25 SMART QUESTIONS TO ASK YOUR INTERVIEWER

5. Show Long-term Interest

Ask questions that demonstrate you're thinking about a long-term future with the company.

Example: "How does the company support employees who are interested in transitioning between departments or taking on leadership roles over time?"

Conclusion

Asking thoughtful, well-prepared questions is a crucial part of the interview process. It not only helps you gather valuable information about the role and company but also demonstrates your genuine interest, preparation, and strategic thinking. By using these 25 smart questions as a starting point and adapting them to your specific situation, you can engage in meaningful dialogue with your interviewer and leave a lasting, positive impression. Remember, an interview is a two-way street – it's your opportunity to evaluate the company and role as much as it is theirs to evaluate you. Asking the right questions helps ensure that you have the information you need to make an informed decision about your career move.

18. The Ultimate Interview Toolkit: Checklist, Power Words, and Preparation Tips

A successful interview requires thorough preparation. This comprehensive toolkit provides you with a pre-interview checklist, powerful words to enhance your responses, and essential preparation tips to ensure you're ready to make a strong impression.

Pre-Interview Checklist

1. Research the Company:
   ☐ Company history and mission
   ☐ Recent news and developments
   ☐ Products or services
   ☐ Competitors
   ☐ Company culture and values

2. Understand the Role:
   ☐ Review job description thoroughly
   ☐ Identify key skills and qualifications required
   ☐ Research typical responsibilities for the position

3. Prepare Your Responses:
   ☐ Practice answers to common interview questions

☐ Develop STAR (Situation, Task, Action, Result) stories
☐ Prepare questions to ask the interviewer

4. Document Preparation:
   ☐ Multiple copies of your resume
   ☐ List of references
   ☐ Portfolio of work (if applicable)
   ☐ Pen and notepad

5. Appearance:
   ☐ Choose and prepare appropriate interview attire
   ☐ Ensure clothes are clean and pressed
   ☐ Plan grooming (haircut, manicure, etc.)

6. Logistics:
   ☐ Confirm interview time and location
   ☐ Plan your route and transportation
   ☐ Aim to arrive 10-15 minutes early

7. Technology Check (for virtual interviews):
   ☐ Test your internet connection
   ☐ Check camera and microphone
   ☐ Ensure your background is professional
   ☐ Close unnecessary applications on your device

8. Mental Preparation:
   ☐ Review your career goals
   ☐ Practice relaxation techniques
   ☐ Get a good night's sleep

Power Words to Enhance Your Responses

Incorporating powerful, action-oriented words into your responses can make your answers more impactful and memorable. Here's a list of power words categorized by common interview themes:

1. Leadership:
   - Spearheaded
   - Orchestrated
   - Mentored
   - Delegated
   - Empowered

2. Problem-Solving:
   - Resolved
   - Troubleshot
   - Innovated
   - Streamlined
   - Optimized

3. Achievement:
   - Accomplished
   - Exceeded
   - Outperformed
   - Surpassed
   - Pioneered

4. Teamwork:
   - Collaborated
   - Facilitated
   - Coordinated
   - Partnered
   - Synergized

5. Innovation:
   - Redesigned

- Conceptualized
- Transformed
- Revolutionized
- Overhauled

6. Efficiency:
   - Accelerated
   - Maximized
   - Consolidated
   - Economized
   - Expedited

7. Communication:
   - Negotiated
   - Persuaded
   - Articulated
   - Mediated
   - Influenced

8. Analysis:
   - Evaluated
   - Assessed
   - Investigated
   - Diagnosed
   - Scrutinized

9. Growth:
   - Expanded
   - Cultivated
   - Amplified
   - Augmented
   - Bolstered

10. Initiative:
   - Launched
   - Initiated
   - Spearheaded
   - Implemented
   - Established

Essential Preparation Tips

1. Master Your Elevator Pitch
   Craft a concise, compelling summary of your professional background and career goals. Practice delivering it smoothly in 30-60 seconds.

2. Conduct Mock Interviews
   Enlist a friend or mentor to conduct practice interviews. Request honest feedback on your responses, body language, and overall presentation.

3. Research Your Interviewers
   If possible, learn about your interviewers' backgrounds. This can help you establish rapport and tailor your responses to their perspectives.

4. Prepare for Different Interview Styles
   Familiarize yourself with various interview formats (behavioral, case, technical) and practice accordingly.

5. Develop a Consistent Personal Brand
   Ensure your resume, LinkedIn profile, and interview responses present a cohesive professional narrative.

6. Quantify Your Achievements
   Wherever possible, use specific numbers and percentages to illustrate your accomplishments.

18. THE ULTIMATE INTERVIEW TOOLKIT: CHECKLIST, POWER WORDS,...

7. Prepare for Tough Questions
Anticipate and practice responding to challenging questions about gaps in employment, weaknesses, or reasons for leaving previous jobs.

8. Master the STAR Method
For behavioral questions, structure your responses using the Situation, Task, Action, Result format to provide comprehensive, focused answers.

9. Cultivate a Growth Mindset
Prepare examples that demonstrate your ability to learn from challenges and adapt to new situations.

10. Develop Industry Insights
Stay informed about current trends, challenges, and innovations in your industry to demonstrate your engagement and forward-thinking approach.

11. Prepare Thoughtful Questions
Develop insightful questions about the role, company, and industry to ask your interviewer, demonstrating your genuine interest and preparation.

12. Practice Active Listening
During the interview, focus on truly understanding the questions asked. Don't hesitate to ask for clarification if needed.

13. Refine Your Body Language
Practice maintaining good posture, making appropriate eye contact, and using hand gestures effectively to enhance your verbal communication.

14. Prepare a Closing Statement
Develop a brief closing statement that reiterates your interest in the position and summarizes why you're the ideal candidate.

15. Plan Your Follow-Up

Prepare a template for a post-interview thank-you email, which you can customize and send promptly after the interview.

16. Manage Interview Anxiety
Develop strategies to manage nerves, such as deep breathing exercises or positive visualization techniques.

17. Tailor Your Responses
Customize your answers to align with the specific needs and culture of the company you're interviewing with.

18. Prepare Salary Expectations
Research industry standards for the role and prepare a salary range based on your experience and the position's requirements.

19. Develop a Portfolio
If applicable to your field, prepare a portfolio of your work to showcase your skills and achievements visually.

20. Practice Video Interview Etiquette
For virtual interviews, practice looking directly at the camera, eliminating background distractions, and projecting energy through the screen.

Conclusion

This comprehensive interview toolkit equips you with the essential elements needed to excel in your interview. The pre-interview checklist ensures you've covered all bases in your preparation, from company research to logistical details. The power words provide a vocabulary to make your responses more dynamic and impactful, allowing you to articulate your experiences and skills with precision and force.

The preparation tips offer a roadmap for thorough interview readiness, cov-

18. THE ULTIMATE INTERVIEW TOOLKIT: CHECKLIST, POWER WORDS,...

ering everything from crafting your personal brand to managing interview anxiety. By diligently working through each element of this toolkit, you'll enter your interview with confidence, preparedness, and the ability to present yourself as the ideal candidate for the position.

Remember, effective interview preparation is about more than just rehearsing answers; it's about developing a deep understanding of your own professional narrative, the needs of the company, and how you can bridge the two. With this toolkit as your guide, you'll be well-equipped to navigate the interview process successfully and move closer to securing your desired position.

19. Overcoming Interview Anxiety: Techniques for Staying Calm and Confident

Interview anxiety is a common experience that can affect even the most qualified candidates. While some nervousness is normal and can even be beneficial, excessive anxiety can hinder your performance. This chapter explores various techniques to manage interview anxiety, helping you stay calm and confident throughout the process.

Understanding Interview Anxiety

Interview anxiety typically stems from:

1. Fear of the unknown
2. Pressure to perform
3. Past negative experiences
4. Self-doubt or imposter syndrome
5. High stakes (e.g., dream job, career change)

Recognizing the signs of anxiety (rapid heartbeat, sweating, shortness of breath) is the first step in managing it effectively.

Preparation Techniques

19. OVERCOMING INTERVIEW ANXIETY: TECHNIQUES FOR STAYING...

1. Thorough Research

Anxiety often comes from feeling unprepared. Conduct extensive research on the company, role, and industry to boost your confidence.

2. Practice, Practice, Practice

Conduct mock interviews with friends or mentors. The more you practice, the more comfortable you'll feel during the actual interview.

3. Visualize Success

Spend time visualizing a successful interview. Imagine yourself answering questions confidently and building rapport with the interviewer.

4. Prepare a 'Cheat Sheet'

Create a one-page document with key points about your experience, achievements, and questions for the interviewer. Review this before the interview to reinforce your preparation.

5. Plan Your Journey

If it's an in-person interview, plan your route in advance and aim to arrive 15-20 minutes early. This buffer time allows you to compose yourself and reduces transit-related stress.

Physical Techniques for Anxiety Management

1. Deep Breathing Exercises

Practice deep, diaphragmatic breathing to activate your body's relaxation response:
   - Inhale slowly through your nose for 4 counts
   - Hold for 4 counts
   - Exhale slowly through your mouth for 4 counts
   - Repeat 5-10 times

2. Progressive Muscle Relaxation

Systematically tense and then relax different muscle groups to release physical tension:
  - Start with your toes and work your way up to your face
  - Tense each muscle group for 5 seconds, then release for 10 seconds
  - Focus on the sensation of relaxation in each area

3. Power Posing

Adopt confident body postures for a few minutes before the interview to boost confidence and reduce stress hormones:
  - Stand tall with your feet apart and hands on your hips
  - Sit with your arms behind your head and feet on the desk
  - Hold these poses for 2-3 minutes

4. Exercise

Engage in light exercise on the day of the interview to release endorphins and reduce stress:
  - Take a brisk walk
  - Do some light stretching or yoga
  - Avoid intense workouts that might leave you fatigued

5. Proper Nutrition and Hydration
  - Eat a balanced meal before the interview to stabilize blood sugar
  - Stay hydrated, but avoid excessive caffeine
  - Consider calming herbs like chamomile tea

Cognitive Techniques

1. Positive Self-Talk

Replace negative thoughts with positive affirmations:
  - Instead of "I'm not qualified," think "I have unique experiences to offer"
  - Replace "I'll mess this up" with "I'm well-prepared and capable"

2. Reframe Anxiety as Excitement

Anxiety and excitement have similar physiological responses. Try relabeling your anxiety as excitement about the opportunity.

3. Mindfulness Meditation

Practice being present in the moment to reduce anxiety about future outcomes:
  - Focus on your breath or physical sensations
  - Acknowledge thoughts without judgment and let them pass
  - Start with short sessions (5-10 minutes) and gradually increase

4. Cognitive Restructuring

Challenge and reframe anxious thoughts:
  - Identify the anxious thought (e.g., "I'll blank out during the interview")
  - Evaluate its validity ("Has this happened before? How likely is it really?")
  - Replace with a more balanced thought ("I've prepared well and can handle unexpected questions")

5. Focus on Your Purpose

Remind yourself why you're pursuing this opportunity. Connecting with your larger goals can help put the interview into perspective.

In-the-Moment Techniques

1. Grounding Exercises

If anxiety spikes during the interview, try the 5-4-3-2-1 technique:
  - Identify 5 things you can see
  - 4 things you can touch
  - 3 things you can hear
  - 2 things you can smell
  - 1 thing you can taste

2. Pause and Breathe

Before answering a question, take a brief pause and a deep breath. This gives you time to compose your thoughts and reduces rushed, anxious responses.

3. Use Anchoring

Choose a physical object (like a ring or watch) to serve as an 'anchor'. When feeling anxious, touch this object to remind yourself to stay calm and centered.

4. Maintain Good Posture

Sit up straight with your shoulders back. Good posture can make you feel more confident and helps regulate breathing.

5. Stay Hydrated

Keep a glass of water nearby. Taking small sips can help you pause and collect your thoughts.

Post-Interview Anxiety Management

1. Self-Compassion

Treat yourself kindly after the interview. Avoid harsh self-criticism and acknowledge that you did your best.

2. Relaxation Reward

Plan a relaxing activity after the interview as a reward for your efforts.

3. Reflective Journaling

Write about your interview experience, focusing on what went well and areas for improvement.

4. Redirect Focus

After the interview, engage in activities that take your mind off waiting for the outcome.

19. OVERCOMING INTERVIEW ANXIETY: TECHNIQUES FOR STAYING...

Building Long-Term Resilience

1. Develop a Growth Mindset
   View interviews as opportunities for learning and growth, regardless of the outcome.

2. Regular Self-Care
   Maintain ongoing stress-management practices like exercise, meditation, or hobbies.

3. Seek Professional Help if Needed
   If anxiety significantly impacts your life, consider speaking with a therapist or counselor.

4. Gradual Exposure
   Seek out low-stakes interview opportunities (informational interviews, networking events) to build confidence over time.

5. Continuous Learning
   Stay updated in your field to boost confidence in your professional knowledge.

Special Considerations for Different Interview Formats

1. Video Interviews
   - Test technology in advance to reduce tech-related anxiety
   - Look at the camera to simulate eye contact
   - Use sticky notes around your screen for key points

2. Phone Interviews
   - Stand up or walk around to release nervous energy
   - Keep your resume and notes visible
   - Smile while speaking to project confidence in your voice

3. Panel Interviews
   - Make eye contact with all panel members
   - Take brief notes to give yourself short mental breaks
   - Remember that multiple interviewers often means a more conversational style

Conclusion

Interview anxiety is a common challenge, but it doesn't have to derail your performance. By implementing a combination of preparation techniques, physical relaxation methods, cognitive strategies, and in-the-moment tactics, you can effectively manage your anxiety and showcase your true potential.

Remember, some level of nervousness is normal and can even enhance your performance by keeping you alert and focused. The goal is not to eliminate anxiety entirely, but to channel it productively. With practice and persistence, you can develop a toolkit of anxiety management techniques that work best for you.

Approach each interview as an opportunity for growth and learning. Over time, as you gain more experience and refine your anxiety management strategies, you'll find yourself feeling increasingly confident and composed in interview situations. This newfound confidence will not only improve your interview performance but will also serve you well throughout your professional journey.

20. Building Your Personal Brand: Resume, Cover Letter, and Online Presence

In today's competitive job market, building a strong personal brand is crucial for standing out to potential employers. Your personal brand is the unique combination of skills, experiences, and personality that you want others to see. It's communicated through various channels, primarily your resume, cover letter, and online presence. This chapter will guide you through effectively crafting each of these elements to create a cohesive and compelling personal brand.

1. Crafting an Impactful Resume

Your resume is often the first impression you make on a potential employer. It should be clear, concise, and tailored to the job you're applying for.

Key Elements of an Effective Resume:

a) Strong Summary or Objective Statement
   Begin with a brief, powerful statement that encapsulates your professional identity and career goals.

b) Relevant Work Experience
   List your work history in reverse chronological order. Focus on achieve-

ments rather than just responsibilities, using action verbs and quantifiable results.

c) Skills Section
   Highlight both hard and soft skills relevant to the position you're seeking.

d) Education and Certifications
   Include your educational background and any relevant certifications or additional training.

e) Achievements and Awards
   Showcase any significant professional accomplishments or recognition.

Tips for Resume Writing:

- Tailor your resume for each job application
    - Use keywords from the job description
    - Keep it concise (typically 1-2 pages)
    - Use a clean, professional format
    - Proofread meticulously for errors

2. Crafting a Compelling Cover Letter

Your cover letter is an opportunity to expand on your resume and show how your experiences align with the job requirements.

Key Elements of an Effective Cover Letter:

a) Strong Opening
   Begin with a hook that grabs the reader's attention and expresses your enthusiasm for the role.

b) Alignment with Company Values

20. BUILDING YOUR PERSONAL BRAND: RESUME, COVER LETTER, AND...

Demonstrate your understanding of the company's mission and how you align with it.

c) Relevant Achievements
Highlight 2-3 key achievements that directly relate to the job requirements.

d) Unique Value Proposition
Clearly articulate what sets you apart from other candidates.

e) Call to Action
Conclude with a strong statement expressing your interest in moving forward in the process.

Tips for Cover Letter Writing:

- Customize each cover letter for the specific job and company
    - Keep it concise (typically one page)
    - Use a professional tone while letting your personality shine through
    - Address it to a specific person if possible
    - Proofread carefully for errors and clarity

3. Building a Strong Online Presence

In the digital age, your online presence is a crucial part of your personal brand. It can reinforce the image you present in your resume and cover letter, and provide additional depth to your professional profile.

Key Elements of a Strong Online Presence:

a) LinkedIn Profile
Your LinkedIn profile should be a more comprehensive version of your resume.

- Use a professional photo
    - Write a compelling headline and summary
    - Detail your work experience, focusing on achievements
    - List relevant skills and get endorsements
    - Gather recommendations from colleagues and supervisors
    - Engage with content in your industry

b) Professional Website or Portfolio
Consider creating a personal website or online portfolio, especially if you're in a creative field.

- Showcase your best work
    - Include a professional bio
    - Provide contact information
    - Ensure the design reflects your personal brand

c) Twitter/X or Industry-Specific Platforms
Use social media platforms relevant to your industry to engage in professional discussions and share insights.

- Share industry news and your thoughts on it
    - Engage with thought leaders in your field
    - Maintain a professional tone
    - Be consistent in your posting schedule

d) GitHub (for tech professionals)
If you're in a technical field, maintain an active GitHub profile showcasing your coding projects and contributions.

Tips for Managing Your Online Presence:

- Ensure consistency across all platforms
    - Regularly update your profiles

20. BUILDING YOUR PERSONAL BRAND: RESUME, COVER LETTER, AND...

- Be mindful of your digital footprint – assume everything you post online is public
- Google yourself regularly to monitor your online presence
- Consider setting up Google Alerts for your name

4. Creating a Cohesive Personal Brand

Your personal brand should be consistent across your resume, cover letter, and online presence. Here's how to ensure cohesion:

a) Develop Your Brand Statement
Create a clear, concise statement that defines who you are professionally, what you excel at, and what you're passionate about.

b) Identify Your Unique Selling Proposition (USP)
Determine what sets you apart from others in your field. This could be a unique combination of skills, a particular achievement, or a specific perspective you bring to your work.

c) Use Consistent Language
Employ the same key terms and phrases across all your branding materials. This reinforces your personal brand and makes it more memorable.

d) Maintain Visual Consistency
Use the same professional photo across platforms. If you have a personal logo or color scheme, use it consistently.

e) Align Your Story
Ensure that the narrative of your professional journey is consistent across all platforms, while allowing each to showcase different aspects of your experience and personality.

5. Leveraging Your Personal Brand in the Job Search

Once you've built a strong personal brand, use it effectively in your job search:

a) Networking

Use your brand to make meaningful connections. Attend industry events, join professional associations, and engage in online forums relevant to your field.

b) Informational Interviews

Reach out to professionals in your desired field or company. Your clear personal brand will make these requests more compelling.

c) Job Applications

Ensure that your personal brand shines through in every job application. Tailor your materials to each opportunity while maintaining your core brand identity.

d) Interviews

In interviews, reinforce the personal brand you've established through your application materials. Be prepared to elaborate on the experiences and skills you've highlighted.

e) Follow-Up

After interviews or networking events, follow up with personalized messages that reinforce your brand and the value you can bring to an organization.

Conclusion

Building a strong personal brand through your resume, cover letter, and online presence is an ongoing process. It requires self-reflection, consistency, and regular updates as your career evolves. By presenting a cohesive, authentic, and compelling personal brand, you increase your visibility to potential employers and position yourself as a valuable asset in your field.

Remember, your personal brand should be a true reflection of your professional self. It's not about creating a false image, but about effectively communicating your genuine strengths, experiences, and aspirations. With a well-crafted personal brand, you'll be better equipped to navigate your career journey and seize opportunities that align with your professional goals.

Conclusion: Your Journey to Interview Excellence

As we conclude this comprehensive guide to mastering job interviews, it's important to recognize that achieving interview excellence is not a destination, but a journey. The skills and strategies you've learned are not just for landing your next job; they're tools for ongoing career development and professional growth. Let's recap the key elements of your journey to interview excellence and discuss how to maintain and evolve these skills throughout your career.

1. Continuous Learning and Adaptation

The job market and interview processes are constantly evolving. To maintain interview excellence:

- Stay updated on industry trends and new interview techniques
    - Regularly revisit and update your interview preparation strategies
    - Seek feedback after interviews, whether successful or not, to identify areas for improvement
    - Adapt your approach based on changing market demands and company cultures

2. Building Confidence Through Preparation

CONCLUSION: YOUR JOURNEY TO INTERVIEW EXCELLENCE

Confidence is key in interviews, and it comes from thorough preparation:

- Regularly update your knowledge of your industry and potential employers
    - Practice articulating your experiences and skills clearly and concisely
    - Develop and maintain a 'success journal' to remind yourself of your achievements
    - Engage in continuous skill development to stay competitive in your field

3. Mastering the Art of Storytelling

Your ability to tell compelling stories about your professional experiences is crucial:

- Continuously refine your STAR (Situation, Task, Action, Result) stories
    - Seek opportunities to present or speak publicly to enhance your narrative skills
    - Practice adapting your stories for different contexts and audiences
    - Regularly reflect on new experiences to add to your repertoire of professional anecdotes

4. Cultivating Emotional Intelligence

Emotional intelligence is increasingly valued in the workplace:

- Practice self-awareness and self-regulation in various professional settings
    - Seek feedback on your interpersonal skills and work on areas of improvement
    - Develop your ability to read and respond to others' emotions and non-verbal cues
    - Engage in activities that enhance empathy and social skills

5. Embracing a Growth Mindset

Approach every interview, regardless of the outcome, as a learning opportunity:

- View challenges as opportunities for growth rather than obstacles
    - Be open to constructive criticism and use it to improve
    - Celebrate small wins and learn from setbacks
    - Continuously set new goals for your professional development

6. Networking and Relationship Building

Excellence in interviewing extends to all professional interactions:

- Maintain and expand your professional network
    - Practice your interview skills in informational interviews and networking events
    - Seek mentorship opportunities, both as a mentee and mentor
    - Engage in industry forums and discussions to stay connected and informed

7. Tailoring Your Approach

Remember that each interview is unique:

- Continue to refine your ability to research companies and roles thoroughly
    - Practice adapting your communication style to different interviewers and company cultures
    - Develop flexibility in your responses to handle various interview formats and questions

8. Managing Stress and Anxiety

Interview excellence includes managing your mental and emotional state:

CONCLUSION: YOUR JOURNEY TO INTERVIEW EXCELLENCE

- Regularly practice stress-management techniques like meditation or deep breathing
    - Maintain a healthy work-life balance to build overall resilience
    - Seek support when needed, whether from mentors, peers, or professionals
    - Develop pre-interview rituals that help you center and focus

9. Staying Authentic

While mastering interview techniques is important, maintaining authenticity is crucial:

- Regularly reflect on your values, goals, and passions
    - Ensure your interview responses align with your true self
    - Practice articulating your unique value proposition confidently
    - Be honest about your strengths and areas for growth

10. Leveraging Technology

Stay adept at navigating technology in the interview process:

- Keep your online profiles and digital portfolio updated
    - Stay familiar with various video conferencing platforms
    - Practice virtual interview techniques regularly
    - Be aware of emerging technologies in recruitment and prepare accordingly

11. Developing Critical Thinking and Problem-Solving Skills

Showcase your ability to think on your feet:

- Engage in activities that enhance your analytical skills
    - Practice answering unexpected or challenging questions
    - Develop your ability to break down complex problems in interviews

- Stay informed about current events and industry challenges to discuss thoughtfully

12. Maintaining Professional Etiquette

Excellence in interviewing includes impeccable professional conduct:

- Continuously refine your communication skills, both verbal and written
    - Stay up-to-date on business etiquette in various cultural contexts
    - Practice promptness and follow-through in all professional interactions
    - Maintain a professional image across all platforms and interactions

13. Giving Back and Sharing Knowledge

As you gain expertise in interviewing:

- Offer to conduct mock interviews for peers or junior professionals
    - Share your insights and experiences with others in your network
    - Consider mentoring others in career development
    - Contribute to professional forums or write articles on interview best practices

14. Balancing Confidence and Humility

Strive for a balance that showcases your abilities while remaining open to learning:

- Practice articulating your achievements without arrogance
    - Demonstrate curiosity and a willingness to learn in every interaction
    - Be confident in your skills while acknowledging areas for growth
    - Show appreciation for the experiences and insights of others

15. Continuous Self-Assessment

CONCLUSION: YOUR JOURNEY TO INTERVIEW EXCELLENCE

Regularly evaluate your interview skills and career progress:

- Set periodic goals for improving specific aspects of your interview performance
    - Seek regular feedback from trusted colleagues or mentors
    - Reflect on each interview experience and document lessons learned
    - Adjust your career objectives and interview strategies as your professional journey evolves

Conclusion

Your journey to interview excellence is an integral part of your overall professional development. The skills you've developed – from articulating your value proposition to managing stress under pressure – are valuable not just in interviews but in many aspects of your career.

Remember that true interview excellence is not about perfection, but about continuous improvement and authentic self-presentation. It's about being well-prepared, adaptable, and genuine in your interactions. As you move forward in your career, continue to refine these skills, stay open to new learning, and approach each interview as an opportunity for growth.

The confidence and competence you develop through this journey will not only serve you well in interviews but will enhance your overall professional presence. You'll find that the skills of self-reflection, clear communication, and strategic thinking that are crucial in interviews are equally valuable in day-to-day work situations, presentations, and leadership roles.

Embrace this journey with enthusiasm and persistence. Each interview, each interaction, is a step forward in your professional growth. Stay curious, remain adaptable, and continue to invest in your personal and professional development. With these tools and mindset, you're well-equipped to navigate the challenges and opportunities of your career path, turning each interview into a stepping stone towards your professional aspirations.

Chapter 23

Bonus Section:

1. Mock Interview Scripts

Mock Interview Script #1: Entry-Level Marketing Position

Interviewer: "Tell me about yourself and why you're interested in this marketing role."

Candidate: "I'm a recent graduate with a degree in Marketing from XYZ University. During my studies, I developed a strong foundation in marketing principles and gained practical experience through internships at local businesses. I'm particularly interested in digital marketing and have completed several online courses in SEO and social media marketing. I'm excited about this role because it aligns perfectly with my skills and your company's focus on innovative digital strategies."

Interviewer: "Can you describe a marketing campaign you've worked on and its results?"

Candidate: "During my internship at ABC Company, I assisted in developing a social media campaign for a new product launch. I was responsible for creating engaging content for Instagram and Facebook. The campaign resulted in a 30% increase in follower engagement and contributed to a 15% boost in sales during the first month of the product's release."

Interviewer: "How do you stay updated with the latest marketing trends?"

Candidate: "I follow several marketing blogs and podcasts, including HubSpot and Marketing Over Coffee. I'm also active in marketing groups on LinkedIn where professionals share insights and discuss industry trends. Additionally, I attend webinars and virtual conferences when possible to learn from industry experts."

Mock Interview Script #2: Mid-Level Software Developer Position

Interviewer: "Can you walk me through your experience with agile development methodologies?"

Candidate: "I've been working in agile environments for the past five years. In my current role, I'm part of a Scrum team where we work in two-week sprints. I'm experienced in daily stand-ups, sprint planning, and retrospectives. I've also taken on the role of Scrum Master for several sprints, which has given me a broader perspective on agile project management."

Interviewer: "Describe a challenging bug you encountered and how you resolved it."

Candidate: "In a recent project, we encountered a memory leak in our mobile app that was causing crashes for users with older devices. I led the debugging effort, using profiling tools to identify the source of the leak. It turned out to be related to how we were handling image caching. I implemented a more efficient caching mechanism that resolved the issue and improved overall app performance by 20%."

Interviewer: "How do you approach learning new technologies or programming languages?"

Candidate: "I'm a firm believer in continuous learning. When approaching a new technology, I start by reading the official documentation and following tutorials. Then, I like to build small projects to get hands-on experience. For example, when learning React, I built a simple task management app. I also leverage online communities like Stack Overflow and GitHub discussions to learn from others' experiences and best practices."

1. Interview Anxiety Management Techniques

a) Breathing Exercises:

- 4-7-8 Technique: Inhale for 4 counts, hold for 7 counts, exhale for 8

counts.
- Box Breathing: Inhale for 4 counts, hold for 4 counts, exhale for 4 counts, hold for 4 counts.

b) Visualization:

- Imagine yourself confidently answering questions and building rapport with the interviewer.
- Visualize a successful outcome and how you'll feel afterward.

c) Progressive Muscle Relaxation:

- Systematically tense and relax different muscle groups, starting from your toes and moving up to your head.

d) Positive Self-Talk:

- Replace negative thoughts with positive affirmations.
- Examples: "I am well-prepared for this interview" or "I have valuable skills to offer."

e) Mindfulness Techniques:

- Practice being present in the moment to reduce anxiety about future outcomes.
- Focus on your senses: What can you see, hear, feel, smell, and taste right now?

1. Digital Interview Portfolio Guide

a) Choose the Right Platform:

- Options include personal websites (e.g., WordPress, Wix), portfolio sites (e.g., Behance, Dribbble), or LinkedIn.

b) Organize Your Work:

- Group projects by category or skill.
- Include a mix of professional work, personal projects, and volunteer experiences.

c) Showcase Your Best Work:

- Quality over quantity – select your most impressive and relevant projects.
- Include detailed descriptions of your role, challenges faced, and outcomes achieved.

d) Make It Visually Appealing:

- Use a clean, professional design.
- Ensure easy navigation and mobile responsiveness.

e) Include a Strong About Me Section:

- Write a compelling bio that highlights your unique value proposition.
- Include a professional photo and contact information.

f) Incorporate Testimonials:

- Include quotes from clients, colleagues, or supervisors praising your work.

g) Keep It Updated:

- Regularly add new projects and remove outdated ones.
- Ensure all information is current and accurate.

CHAPTER 23

1. Exclusive Online Resources and Updates

a) Interview Preparation Websites:

- Glassdoor.com: Company reviews and interview questions.
- InterviewBit.com: Practice coding interviews.
- BigInterview.com: AI-powered interview practice.

b) Industry News and Trends:

- LinkedIn News: Customized news feed for your industry.
- Industry-specific publications (e.g., TechCrunch for tech, AdAge for marketing).

c) Skill Development Platforms:

- Coursera.org: Online courses from top universities.
- Udemy.com: Wide range of professional development courses.
- Skillshare.com: Creative and business skills courses.

d) Networking Resources:

- Meetup.com: Find professional networking events in your area.
- Eventbrite.com: Discover industry conferences and webinars.

e) Career Advice Podcasts:

- "Career Tools" by Manager Tools
- "Find Your Dream Job" by Mac's List

f) Salary Information:

- Salary.com: Comprehensive salary data for various positions.

- Payscale.com: Personalized salary reports.

g) Resume and Cover Letter Tools:

- ResumGenius.com: Resume builder and templates.
- Grammarly.com: Writing assistance and proofreading.

h) Professional Development Communities:

- Reddit.com/r/jobs: Career advice and job search tips.
- Quora.com: Q&A platform for career-related queries.

Remember to regularly check these resources for updates and new features. Stay engaged with professional communities and forums to get the latest insights and advice on job searching and interview

YOU CAN ALSO READ MY OTHER BOOK (HOW TO ACE AN INTERVIEW) TO BRIGHTEN UP YOUR MIND FURTHER INTO INSIDER SECRETS THAT WILL HELP YOUR NAIL YOUR DREAM JOB.

GO AHEAD AND SHINE

www.ingramcontent.com/pod-product-compliance
Lightning Source LLC
Chambersburg PA
CBHW071923210526
45479CB00002B/529